REFLECTING ON NANA

A radical challenge to the view of *Nana* as the story of an old-fashioned *femme fatale*, *Reflecting on Nana* presents an alternative feminist reading. Bernice Chitnis claims Nana as a heroine who manages to manipulate patriarchy and to achieve her own kind of victory over it, overturning the traditional social order of male domination and offering an alternative.

For Zola, courtesans were powerful women – much more so than wives or daughters. In Nana, he created a character who asserts her right to choose, standing both for women's dignity and human dignity. From her position she can view men as unenlightened bores who have to learn from experience that women have different priorities from men, have alternative experiences, and possess the full range of human characteristics. In creating such a character, Zola struggled to come to terms with his own disturbing vision – a creation he both admired and feared.

Reflecting on Nana takes a radical new approach to a well-known and well-loved work. It will appeal to students of women's studies, French studies, literature and cultural history, and to anyone who has read and enjoyed Zola's novel.

HEROINES?

Certain fictional women have become part of western mythology. They are the stars of novels, films, radio and TV programmes, which have caught the imagination of generations of women. What is the secret of their magnetism?

This new feminist series about literary heroines investigates their lasting appeal. Each writer explores her chosen heroine's relationships with other characters in the novel, with her own author, with readers past and present, and lastly with herself. These characters all touch chords of reality for us. By their very 'ordinariness' they demonstrate that, in the most general feminist sense, all women are heroines.

For general readers as well as students, these concise, elegantly written books will delight all lovers – and even haters – of the original classics.

Titles in the series include:

Mary Evans *Reflecting on Anna Karenina*

Pat Macpherson *Reflecting on Jane Eyre*

Rebecca O'Rourke *Reflecting on The Well of Loneliness*

Pat Macpherson *Reflecting on The Bell Jar*

Marion Shaw and Sabine Vanacker *Reflecting on Miss Marple*

BERNICE CHITNIS

REFLECTING ON NANA

London and New York

First published in 1991
by Routledge
11 New Fetter Lane, London EC4P 4EE

Simultaneously published in the USA and Canada
by Routledge
a division of Routledge, Chapman and Hall Inc.
29 West 35th Street, New York, NY 10001

Typeset by LaserScript, Mitcham, Surrey.
Printed in Great Britain by Cox & Wyman Ltd, Reading

British Library Cataloguing in Publication Data
Chitnis, Bernice *1942-*
Reflecting on Nana. – (Heroines?).
1. Fiction in French. Zola, Emile, 1840–1902
I. Title II. Series
843.8

Library of Congress Cataloging in Publication Data
Chitnis, Bernice, 1942-
Reflecting on Nana/Bernice Chitnis.
p. cm. – (Heroines?)
Includes bibliographical references.
1. Zola, Emile, 1840–1902. Nana. 2. Feminism and literature –
– France – History – 19th century. 3. Heroines in literature.
I. Title. II. Series
PQ2510.C47 1991
843′.8 – dc20 90-49426
CIP

ISBN 0–415–04134–1

TO MY FATHER AND IN MEMORY
OF MY MOTHER

CONTENTS

ACKNOWLEDGEMENTS

I WISH to thank above all for his loving support and encouragement my husband, Anand Chitnis, and, for their affectionate patience, our children, Rajendra, Lucia and Xavier. Also Catherine and Michael, Jane and John, for many learnings about relationships. Thank you, too, to Gill Davies, editor of the series, for her certainty that *Nana* would repay reflection. I acknowledge the help of Ann Hamilton with the typing of the manuscript.

I owe a special debt of gratitude to Peter Jimack, whose enthusiasm and support meant much to me during the writing of this book, and whose friendship over nearly twenty years I deeply value.

All page references are from *Nana* by Emile Zola, translated by George Holden (Harmondsworth: Penguin Classics, 1972), copyright © George Holden, 1972. Reproduced by permission of Penguin Books Ltd.

Chapter One

WHO IS NANA? WHAT IS SHE?

THE NAMES of a few characters in literature make the shift from proper to common noun; when they do, it means that their outstanding quality has taken on legendary proportions, universal, archetypal, eternal significance. In French, Nana's name has passed into the demotic where it designates a young woman, but it is not a neutral, value-free term. It is the term that patriarchs use to make a sexist statement. As Mary Daly has pointed out, since the patriarchal God of Genesis named light and dark, earth and sea, and Adam, the first man, named the beasts, flowers and fruits of the earth, naming has been a male prerogative, and it is the meaning which *he* gives the word that abides (Daly 1973: 6). When in the opening pages of *Nana*, Nana's name is on the lips of every male who has come to her début at the *Variétés*, she is being constructed by them. It is a tribal activity. She is the object – literally – of male curiosity, male speculation, as the men take at first a good-humoured and later an aggressive interest in defining her, pinning her down:

> Gentlemen of unimpeachable appearance repeated: 'Nana! Hey, Nana!' People were crushed together, a quarrel broke out at the box-office, and there was a growing clamour caused by the hum of voices calling for Nana, demanding Nana in one of those accesses of silly facetiousness and crude sensuality which take hold of crowds. (26)

Significantly the women at the performance, 'uneasy and

smiling', can only repeat her name 'softly with an air of surprise' (*24*). Who is Nana? What is Nana? The answers which are readily available – that she is 'a slut' (*24*), 'a tart', 'the girl on the corner of the rue de Provence' (*40*) or 'something invented by Bordenave' (*20*), the theatre manager who has recognized the presence of 'It' in Nana and packaged her for public consumption – ensure that the content of the name is negative.

Language seems to need to restock itself constantly in chauvinist put-downs, words which degrade women and prevent them from getting above themselves. The most reliable dictionary sources place the appearance of Nana's name as a common noun around 1949; in an area as fluid as popular usage it is never easy to know what convergence of social and cultural factors may have stirred slumbering recollections of Zola's character, but the *Robert Dictionary* suggests that it was first used in the student milieu where an awareness of Zola's novel would always have been present, and that it passed from there into familiar use. Thus Nana's name is currently on men's lips once again, and the world is full of 'nanas', prostitutes all. The word is an unambiguously hostile and pejorative response to the threat which men believe women pose. It is an attempt to neutralize their power by reifying them, by making them the Enemy, 'The Other'. It is one of the words which polarize humanity into male and female camps, resuming in its two short syllables all the problems of male–female relationships, and affirming male superiority and separateness.

Just as popular usage calls any man who is sexually highly active a Don Juan without concerning itself with the deeper meanings, with what the activities of the superstud tell us about biological, social and existential maleness or with the content and dynamics of his relationships, so most of those who call a woman 'une nana' are not really concerned with what Nana herself actually did or what she stands for. What they retain of her is the image of the *femme fatale*: she conjures up the sense of primitive dread at the awakening of physical desire by which women make their impact on men. At the *Variétés*, Nana's nude appearance on the stage raised the temperature, destroyed composure and caused involuntary tumescence among her male audience who, only minutes earlier, were pushing her name about with such confidence and superiority; by the end of the evening, it was she who dominated them, leaving them subdued and with a sense of loss of well-being. By implication, any 'nana' can do the same, hence the hostility with which she is viewed. But in fact, I think we need to look carefully at the full significance of this male discomfiture for it symbolizes something far worse in the eyes of men. The Larousse dictionary gives among its examples of the word's modern usage one which refers to 'the girls (les nanas) who want to put an end to the dictatorship of the blokes (les mecs)'. I suspect that this aspect of the word – the challenge which it contains to male authority and superiority – is only dimly, subconsciously, available to most of those who use it, and yet it is exactly what Zola spends nearly five hundred pages describing.

In the opening chapter of the novel, Zola places the action on the battlefield. The pattern is adversarial with Nana on stage and the men in the audience confronting one another. Nana is a lone force, the men are many, differing greatly in age and temperament and thus easily seen as universally representative of the male sex. All the details he so scrupulously furnishes about their rank, pedigree, alliances, male bondings, fortunes – the things that matter to patriarchs – and even about the state of their beards, the most obvious secondary sexual characteristic and traditional patriarchal symbol, leave no room for doubt. Zola's thesis is that what Nana accomplishes single-handed in that auditorium is, symbolically, the rout of patriarchy. The fact that the show in which she is playing is 'irreverent nonsense' which sends up traditional morality and values, and that the whole spectacle is watched by the women and children who disport themselves on the painted ceiling reinforces the message that Nana has triumphed over men at the point where they are weakest – in the 'involuntary' surge of erotic desire – and has brought about nothing less than a radical change in social order. It is this situation and the fear it generates which the rest of the novel explores.

It is a characteristic of all the Rougon-Macquart novels, of which *Nana* is the ninth, that they each in their own way ruminate on the problem of profound social disruption. Together they trace the 'natural and social history of a family under the Second Empire' and they follow the lives of a number of interrelated characters over the years between 1852 and 1870 in a variety of settings and over a range of different socio-economic and professional groups. It is a society on the move; industrialization is taking place and its effects are being felt, powerful forces like money, politics, ambition and power have been unleashed and are at work, the gap between rich and poor is being accentuated, and disruption and disconnection of all sorts are in evidence in the shuddering of machines, the explosion of mines, the violence and dissension of strikes and the pain of human relationships. At the heart of each of the novels there is an area of disorder and chaos, and *Nana* is no exception to this general rule. The story may be resumed as that of a poor girl born in Paris just before the beginning of the Second Empire; her early years spent in the horrifying squalor of the slums to the north of the city are recounted in an earlier novel of the series, *L'Assommoir* (1876). The only escape from these circumstances is through prostitution; after a period of uncertain fortunes during which she gives birth to a son, her story is picked up again in the novel which bears her name. Nana's sex appeal has been recognized by a theatre manager, Bordenave, who launches her as a sex symbol in the title role of *The Blonde Venus*; all Paris flocks to see her and soon many upper-class men are competing for her favours. Her rise to fame coincides with the Paris Exhibition of 1867, which was designed to show the greatness of the Empire, and she receives a prestig-ious international guest, the Prince of Scotland, in her theatre dressing-room. Eventually, following a period as the mistress of the wealthy banker Steiner, and an interlude spent with a fellow actor, Fontan, who beats her, she is installed in her own mag-nificent mansion in the newly constructed Avenue de Villiers by Count Muffat, a serious Catholic *pater familias* and a powerful official of the Empress's court, whose attention she has courted, and becomes a brilliant and fabulously wealthy courtesan. Muffat expects her fidelity; in fact, Nana is flagrantly unfaithful to him with other men who ruin themselves socially, morally and financially for her and her massive consumerist needs, and also with a prostitute, Satin, whom she has known since her childhood in the slums, and who introduces her to lesbian love. When Muffat finds her solving a cash-flow problem by sleeping with his father-in-law, he can cope no longer; he collapses and has to be rescued by his spiritual mentor. Nana gets together as much money as she can by selling off all her possessions for phenomenal sums, scores a last triumph on the Paris stage as Melusine, and then disappears to some foreign destination – Cairo? – Russia? – where she finds new patrons willing to satisfy her craving for wealth. Then, (perhaps) running into problems with her latest protector, Nana returns to Paris, contracts smallpox from contact with her son, and dies of it in July 1870 as the Empire enters its own death-throes.

It is essential to see this as Zola presents it, a dynamic process in which Nana explodes on Paris society, releases sexual desire wherever she is seen, breaks into and destroys the elegant, respectable tenor of the life of the Muffat de Beuville family, and with her insatiable consumerist desires and their imperative desire for sex, projects all her wealthy upper-class male admirers towards the abyss, and with them all the values and institutions which they uphold – family, religion and even the Empire itself – in fact, patriarchal society as Zola knew it. Nana's Paris mansion is described as being built over a chasm, and those who do not actually perish in the pit are left to attend her death at the Grand Hotel, awaiting the Empire's surrender to the Prussians and the cataclysm. Erotic energy replaces the throb of the machine and the heat of the workshop in this novel; towards the end, the mansion – but much more than the mansion, Nana's whole achievement – is described by one of the surviving patriarchs in comparison with massive pieces of civil engineering, an aqueduct near Marseilles whose stone arches straddled an abyss, 'a gigantic work which had cost millions of francs and ten years of struggle' (*448*), the new port of Cherbourg, 'with hundreds of men sweating in the sun, while cranes filled the sea with huge lumps of rock, building a wall on which workmen were occasionally crushed into a bloody pulp' (*449*). But Nana's achievement is so much more extraordinary:

> Viewing the fruit of her labours, [Mignon] felt once more the
> sensation of respect he had experienced on a festive evening in
> a sugar-refiner's château. This château had been built for the
> refiner, a palatial edifice of royal splendour which had been paid
> for by a single material – sugar. It was with something else, a tiny
> thing that people laughed at, a little of her delicate nudity – it
> was with this shameful trifle, so powerful that it could move the
> world, that all alone, without workmen and without the aid of
> machines invented by engineers, she had shaken Paris to its
> foundations, and had built up this fortune on the bodies of dead
> men. (*449*)

What comes over clearly from the analogy is, obviously, the size
of Nana's achievement, but also the ease with which she has
accomplished it, and the terrible cost to men: what is so remark-
able is that she has managed to mount such a massive challenge
to traditional social values and set in motion a political and
socio-cultural shift from what was theoretically a position of
profound inferiority. Some mid- and late-nineteenth-century
women may in practice have had a certain amount of room for
manoeuvre, been able to make certain choices, exercised
authority and gained respect from men, as James F. McMillan's
(1981) analysis suggests. For very many women, though, the
situation was bleak. In his book which focuses on women's
protest in Nana's time (1858–89), Patrick Kay Bidelman
describes women's position as an encumbered one: 'A pervasive
masculinisme, underpinned by centuries of monarcho-clerical
influence, had arisen to ensnare women in a complex web of
legal, socioeconomic, and ideological constraints' (Bidelman
1982: 3). Obviously women had no political voice or part in
public life: they were offered a discriminatory education, were
discriminated against and exploited in the workplace, repressed
by the Church, and confined more and more to their homes by
changing concepts of child-rearing and 'the privatization of
family life' (Bidelman 1982: 30). The idea of a 'female disposi-
tion' was widespread, and women were 'deflected', as Bidelman
puts it, into 'playing feminine social sex roles' (and men, in
consequence, into playing masculine social sex roles) 'rather
than both into more multi-faceted androgynous sex-roles'
(Bidelman 1982: 19). Moreover, for centuries past law had

tended, in matters of marriage, conduct and property, to weigh heavily on women, and hopes that legislation passed during the Revolution might improve the situation for all citizens had not been fulfilled, for the male leaders of the movement had turned out to be strongly anti-feminist and protective of their own sex's position. The Napoleonic code of 1804 'locked women into a paper Bastille of legal restrictions' (Bidelman 1982: 4).

In fact the Civil Code reflected Napoleon's attitude to the organization of society; every institution required a leader of unquestioned authority, and while he provided this leadership for France, men as husbands and fathers would provide it for the family: the family was a miniature empire. The main rulings of the Code are well known; a father or husband was invested with authority, and was owed total obedience. Legal marriage, McMillan says, 'foisted nothing less than legal servitude on the married woman' (McMillan 1981: 25), for she could not without her husband's permission maintain a separate residence, seek employment or undertake education. A husband controlled family property and his wife's earnings; he also had full control of the children. The Code certainly targeted women's sexual activities; a foreign woman who married a Frenchman acquired instant French citizenship, a French woman who married a foreigner lost hers; adultery by a wife was punishable by a prison sentence whereas a husband would receive only a fine in most circumstances; a husband could file a maternity suit, but paternity suits could not be filed; a husband could open his wife's mail lest she be planning or having a clandestine relationship; husbands who killed their wives in the act of adultery were allowed to be acquitted. Married women were classified legally alongside minors and ex-convicts, and single women, faced with society's hostility to their position, were hardly better off. Whatever grand idea may have inspired this legislation, it seems self-evident that through its prohibitions runs a deep fear of what women might be capable of.

The legislation of the Napoleonic Code had, moreover, other consequences for women. Jill Harsin points out that the confirmation in the Code of the 'virtual civil non-existence of women under the law' (1985: xviii) made it very easy for the authorities there to dispense with the most basic civil rights of prostitutes and of many working-class women who were not prostitutes. Regulations relating to prostitution were formulated in Paris in order to combat the transmission of syphilis and related diseases. Basically they required all practising prostitutes to register with the authorities, to practise from registered brothels and to submit to regular medical examination. That those who complied with the regulations were called in French *'filles soumises'* is surely significant; though apparently the rules were framed as a public health and safety measure, they can be seen as a fine example of male authoritarianism. 'All the vague fears, tensions, anxiety and misogyny of the nineteenth century got tangled up in the control of prostitution', writes Harsin (1985: xx), and the regulations became a means whereby the male hierarchy of the morals police imposed domination and control particularly on poor women. The razzias which so frighten Nana and Satin in the novel enabled society to punish and rid itself of its impure-female-elements. In chasing them off the streets and into licensed brothels, they made the women invisible. Vaginal and rectal examinations and the close physical scrutiny necessary to determine the presence of scabies and body-lice represent humiliating and intrusive ways of dealing with women; the dangerous conditions in which these procedures were carried out merely reinforced the hatred with which women were regarded. Inevitably the controls extended – accidentally-on-purpose – not only to those who were actually working a beat but also to women living in irregular situations who were easily intimidated and even to innocent bystanders. It all represented a means of placing a sexual curb upon women, while the legalization of prostitution recognized and legitimized male sexual activity and installed a double standard of sexual behaviour, just as the Civil Code did.

One group of women seemed able to avoid the inferiority and subjection of their sisters, and that was the group made up of high-class prostitutes and courtesans. These women – like their fictional counterparts in *Nana* – had often left their homes and family structures far behind them: they were nobody's daughters, and although in a way the status of courtesan may be seen as resembling that of the wife who repays her keep and protection with sexual availability, she was not bound by a formal marriage contract. Protected by powerful patrons, absolved from the need to register with the police, securely set up in their own establishments, exempt from medical examination – which in fact made them a hazard to men – their worst threat was that they could demonstrate that power and authority did not rest unequivocally with the male, and ironically, they did it through sexual activity, that area of operation made so difficult for other women.

It was Zola's experience as a journalist which seems to have convinced him that these women were powerful indeed. From all over Paris he gleaned reports for the columns he contributed to the press between 1868 and 1870 which suggested that in the carnival atmosphere of the declining Empire they were inaugurating new ways of being and behaving which reversed all previous expectations. These anecdotes are widely recognized as having served as the basis for incidents in *Nana*, but they are usually read as mere 'social comment' or picturesque background material. I think they are more significant. In traditional patriarchal society, as Eva Figes explains, prostitutes, who usually came from the lower classes, were used as mere sexual sewers, for pleasure and experience (Figes 1970: 84). What Zola saw and heard tended to suggest that the notion of the sexual education of the young upper-class male had taken on a new meaning, for these women, now numerous powerful *arrivistes* set up in mansions newly built by Baron Haussmann, had relocated money and property, and were imposing their own standards and values. In *La Tribune* on 6 December 1868, Zola wrote:

> I can't open a newspaper without reading some juicy titbit about those ladies who help our young and idle rich towards maturity by ruining them and making them lose their hair. Young B won two or three hundred thousand francs at the gaming tables, and tall C held a housewarming in her delightful Champs Elysées mansion and by eleven o'clock there were three gentlemen under the table. R slapped P who was stealing her clients from her. It's a wonderful world we live in.
>
> (Kanes 1963: 184, my translation)

Once it had been men who fought duels over women for love and honour; now, apparently, women fought over men for money. The old standards now had no currency, and class distinctions seemed to have sunk without trace as Zola recounts how one young aristocrat, a descendant of crusader knights, thought nothing of rescuing women revellers from the morals police without reflecting that he might be contaminated by his association with them; or how another gives a gift of a valuable pair of carriage horses to his mistress in order to consolidate his reputation in the eyes of those who will see her out driving in the Bois de Boulogne. A quite new set of responses was being internalized as men even cultivated their subjection to the women:

> I am much too insignificant a fellow to have ever set foot inside a fashionable boudoir, but I am told that those who frequent them have the sharpest wit. The queens of these little courts have, it seems, the refinements of language and attitude that set one dreaming of the lovely maidens of Athens. They're all in the first flush of youth, glowing with health and beauty. As in fairytales, when they open their mouths, priceless pearls fall from their lips, adorable, exquisite sentiments like 'Sod off', or 'Got twenty louis on you?' which their admirers think can only be suitably rewarded by a gift of horses at twenty five thousand francs the pair.
>
> (Kanes 1963: 185, my translation)

The admiration of the *jeunesse dorée* for the operettas composed by Offenbach, the plots of which are all about weakness and infidelity and make light of the values of family, property and marriage, caused Zola strong indignation because they were all part of the same problem. Not only did they turn their backs on the old values, but also they provided a vehicle for some provocative acting by the leading ladies, designed to enslave men without a proper sense of their own dignity:

> Our gentlemen, our aristocrats live amid gales of idiotic laughter. They applaud Offenbach's and Halévy's nonsense, they make queens out of wretched tightrope dancers who prance about on the stages of theatres like fairground artists. Their

mistresses are doorkeepers' daughters who drag them down to
their own level of expression and feeling.

> (Kanes 1963: 187, my translation)

Even worse, women were encouraged by the clamours which
rewarded a provocative wiggle of the hips to be sexually assaul-
tive: men had even lost the one initiative which was traditionally
theirs:

> Ah, woe! The day a woman gets it into her head to get down on
> all fours and crawl about naked playing at being the bitch who
> has got out will be the day Paris goes mad with admiration.
>> (Heuri Mitterand's introduction to *Nana*
>> in Zola 1961: 1657, my translation)

Women became a special threat when they demonstrated pub-
licly their sexual freedom and readiness, and they unmanned
men whose sexual role was traditionally the dominant, active
one. No wonder that gender confusion was observed by Zola in
its obvious, acute form, transvestitism. Tracing what he called
'The end of the orgy' during the period from February to June
of 1870 in *La Cloche*, Zola describes scenes which remind him of
Petronius's accounts of the scenes of dissolution which accomp-
anied the last stages of the Roman Empire, and in particular
scenes which involve men dressing as women:

> These men borrowed the nifty fingers of ladies' maids to help
> them, their own menservants having declined to compromise
> their dignity by sticking kiss-curls on their masters' foreheads.
> Then, all made up and laced into corsets, puffing their skirts up
> around them, they lounged in chairs with all the dainty airs and
> graces of ladies of pleasure on the look-out for custom.
>> (Kanes 1963: 224, my translation)

In nineteenth-century France dress was gender-specific, and
Zola who evidently had entirely conventional ideas about how
dress and conduct interrelate saw this phenomenon of cross-
dressing as very sinister: 'See how our men are turning into
women', he exclaimed after the reported sighting of 'a young
man dressed in pink – a man in pink, God help us!' This was

tantamount to turning the world upside down. In such circumstances, women might even dress as men; sexual attraction would operate ambiguously and the age of clear sexual distinctions would be no more. The days when men were men were a thing of the past, he concluded.

I have quoted in some detail here in order to allow Zola's anxiety to come over, and to show the fierce irony which translates fear and aggression. At times he distances himself from events, at others, a flash of sensuality, a touch of social snobbery, break through any appearance of objectivity and undermine the writer's stance on the high moral ground and make him sound distinctly anti-feminist. His panic and rigidity even make him sound politically right-wing, which he certainly was not. In fact, it is likely that dealing with these experiences, Zola was coping with an area of pain and distortion in his own personality. Bourgeois, *méridional* and male, working out of a tradition in which men held all the cards, the conduct of high society around him flouted his rooted expectations and challenged his social assumptions. Zola was a deeply serious man by temperament, concerned with social issues and not at all in tune with the frivolous atmosphere of the Second Empire; more seriously, he also suffered for much of his life from what can be seen as dominance-related problems in human relationships. Psychologists who believe that the young male benefits from the presence in his life of a satisfactory male role model would see as significant the fact that Zola lost his father at the age of seven; he may never have achieved the full psychic separation from his mother which is sometimes viewed as a crucial step in the development of 'maleness'. (There is an interesting discussion of this in Ong 1981: 64–7.) It is generally agreed by his biographers that Zola's marriage to Alexandrine Meley landed him with two mothers, and trapped him squarely between them. (See, for example, Wilson 1952: 82–5.) Unable to form a mature affective bond with his wife and to resolve the conflicts in his situation, Zola was plagued with sexual dysfunction, loss of libido and disgust with the sexual act, which never resulted in the conception of a child. A measure of resolution of his difficulties came eventually with the relationship he formed with Jeanne Rozerot, a woman much younger than himself, very much his social and intellectual inferior and of gentle, unassertive temperament, but the fact remains that for years Zola's masculinity and virility were under challenge. It was not, therefore, easy for him to integrate his responses to what he had seen and heard. The women were beautiful but posed a threat: from being poor and powerless, they had become powerful and controlling. The awe and fear he felt at their achievement – the removal of their money from these upper-class men was viewed by Zola as nothing less than castration – interacted uneasily with his resentment of their activities, his sexual anxiety, and his exasperation and even disgust with the men who let the women get away with it. Moreover, how could what looks like a blurring of the clear distinctions between the sexes have been other than an unnerving prospect when the threat was made so much worse by one's own fragile sense of identity? What, after all, might the outcome be if women in general began to behave less like women 'should', or if men generally were to abandon their conventional roles and traditional attitudes? (This issue is discussed further in Heilbrun 1973: ix–xiv.)

Whatever the cost in mental pain, however – and there is ample evidence that Zola suffered from bouts of stress-related illness during the composition of *Nana* – the artistic integrity of Zola the novelist would not let him shy away from depicting in his novel about a high-class prostitute the truth about sexual relationships which had been borne in on Zola the journalist. Sexual activity is always a hazard for the male, as Andrea Dworkin explains:

> During penetration a man's very being is at once both risked and affirmed. Will the female void swallow him up, consume him, engulf and destroy his penis, his whole self? Will the female void contaminate his tenuous maleness with the overwhelming toxicity of its femaleness? Or will he emerge from the terrifying emptiness of the female's anatomical gaping hole intact – his positivity reified because even when inside her, he managed to maintain the polarity of male and female by maintaining the discreteness and integrity of his steel-like rod; his masculinity affirmed because he did not in fact merge with her and in so

doing lose himself, he did not dissolve into her, he did not become her nor did he become like her, he was not subsumed by her?

(Dworkin 1982: 105–6)

Zola would have known the answer to these questions; his understanding was that in the sex act men are not dominant, but are fatally engulfed and absorbed. There was no way of pretending that the relationships which young men of good family made with prostitutes usually ended with the golden-hearted girls backing off, leaving the values of property to prevail. No trace of a Manon Lescaut or a Marguérite Gautier could be seen in the *demi-monde* of the Second Empire as he knew it. Zola conveys the real situation in the clearest possible terms. In sexual relations with Nana, the men do not emerge from the female void whole and unscathed; they find out that there really is such a thing as a *vagina dentata* as she cannibalizes everything which matters to them. As Zola puts it in the preliminary plan, 'Nana eats up gold, swallows up every sort of wealth. . . . Everything she devours; she eats up what people are earning around her in industry, . . . in high positions, in everything that pays.' Accordingly Nana is shown about to swallow Vandeuvres's last château near Amiens (*316*), merciless enough to 'clean a man out with one snap of her teeth' (*434*). She destroys Steiner 'two bites at a time in order to finish the Prussian off more quickly' (*435*), goes through la Faloise's estates eating farm by farm and field by field – 'At every mouthful Nana swallowed an acre' (*436*). The alimentary metaphors convey an unmistakeable message: 'Nana gobbled up [her admirers] one after the other' (*434*). Nana spells the death of fat family acres, proud names, profitable enterprises and business empires, and the doom of capitalism, inherited wealth and patriarchy.

One might expect that fear and resentment might result in the production of a profoundly misogynist novel, but I think that the author's view of Nana is much more complex and ambiguous, and reveals a capacity to look much more closely and with comprehension and even fascination at the anarchy she incarnates. A period of about seven or eight years separates the apocalyptic visions of the decadent Empire from the actual composition of *Nana*, and a crucial event in this busy period of Zola's creative life was the production of *L'Assommoir* in 1876. It is in this novel in which Anna Coupeau, known as Nana, is born and grows up that Zola faces the implications of her existence. Usually *L'Assommoir* is read as a study of poverty and degradation written by a novelist with an acute social conscience, but as I return to it now in order to recapture Nana's beginnings, it looks more and more like a meditation on the themes of patriarchy and authority. They are confronted first of all in connection with the novel's principal female character, Gervaise, later to become Nana's mother, who is seen at the beginning of the novel in desperate circumstances, abandoned by her partner, Lantier, with two small sons and no means of support. She takes in washing to make money, and begins to prosper; she then meets and marries Coupeau, and sets up her own business. Gervaise has all the attributes necessary to make a success of her laundry, to be her own boss and assert her independence and improve her family's status – ability, industry, courage and ambition, and also (significantly) authority. In fact she almost does succeed, but Zola makes her fail: perhaps because he found the idea of her 'emancipation' and success worrying. What prevents her from succeeding is on the one hand her bond with Lantier, her first lover when she was fourteen, and on the other, her relationship with her husband, Coupeau. The bond with Lantier is described as a kind of biological/psychosexual 'imprinting' which clearly supports the notion that the male is master and exerts lifelong influence over 'his' woman: the relationship between husband and wife also posits the supremacy of the male and the dutiful submission of the wife even when he has become a degenerate brute. Zola adduces various reasons for Gervaise's destruction – an unpromising heredity, her appetite for sex and later in the novel, an addiction to alcohol – and their impact is cumulative. But what comes over clearly to me is that sexual relations are the root of what happens to Gervaise. Sex is not really about pleasure, it is about power; there is no better illustration than Gervaise of the phenomenon which Andrea Dworkin describes, in which the phallic mastery of the sex act engenders masochistic female submission and results in female non-identity. Gervaise, increasingly trapped, grows submissive and compliant even to the absorption of her will and personality – needless to say, her business fails and she loses all her confident autonomy.

I do think that Zola engenders our sympathy for her, but at the same time it is the portrayal of Lantier and Coupeau which is fascinating for what it says about the attraction of the macho. They are initially a contrast to one another: Lantier the 'hard man' and Coupeau gentle and considerate, but Coupeau is not left long with these characteristics before an accident of a prophetic nature transforms him. One day, as he is working to repair some pipe-work on a roof near his home, his attention is attracted by his delightful little daughter on the pavement below; he misses his footing and falls to the ground, badly injured. Nana has claimed her first male victim. Once Coupeau has no proper job and no money, and is therefore not a proper man any more, he finds another way of demonstrating his virility by joining the tight-knit male world of the drinking den. It is not that Zola is unaware of the pitfalls of machismo; he surely condemns the father of Lalie Bijard who demonstrates the worst aspects of patriarchal authoritarianism. In his case, mastery on the home front is achieved only by violence; he has already killed his wife and has turned his attention to his eight-year-old female child who has assumed the role of mother and housekeeper. Her passivity and acceptance of his cruelty are haunting, her horrific death the most harrowing event of the novel. On the other hand, another character poses the problem of the biological male who is 'feminine' in personality: Goujet, the physically powerful metalworker, is gentle, unassertive, non-aggressive. As Gervaise's submissive, unforceful admirer, he will not – cannot – take the upper hand and impose himself; in Zola's book he is a loser.

L'Assommoir thus raises all sorts of questions about authority and oppression, masculinity and virility, sex and gender, passivity, acceptance, resistance and violence. The way the novel is written makes Gervaise, Lantier and Coupeau the main focus of interest, but the strength of Zola's obsession with these problems can be judged from the fact that Nana's own story, which runs through as an apparently secondary theme, treats exactly the same questions and even, arguably, takes the debate a stage further. What Zola created in the young Nana we meet in *L'Assommoir* is a character who shows an independent, dominant personality from her earliest days. Her infant naughtiness is shown as indiscipline, an anarchic lack of respect for authority, and emphasis is laid on her leadership of other children:

> Nana ruled this heap of toads; she was a little madam even with girls twice her age and exerted over them the despotic sway of a fully-grown adult.
>
> (*L'Assommoir* in Zola 1961: 519, my translation)

The neighbourhood tomboy in childhood, at thirteen she wears a perpetual air of effrontery. At fifteen, she is a challenge to paternal and maternal authority, to the respect due to tradition, age and infirmity; the young girls of the rue de la Goutte-d'Or, led by Nana, impose themselves on their environment – 'The street belonged to them'. Zola attributes to Nana an inclination to vice, by which he means a precocious interest in sex, but the implication is that she is much more generally out of line. Yet he allows her to remain untameable despite beatings, pleadings and the force of opinion against her. Nana never bonds closely with her mother; Zola makes her eye Gervaise with the harsh but truthful gaze of an adolescent girl who sees her mother as having sold out to the patriarchs. Her decision to leave home for good marks the explicit rejection of all sorts of authority construed as oppression; the structures of her milieu which condemn her to work for a pittance in Titreville's sweatshop where she makes money for male bosses, the conventions of behaviour forced upon young girls by traditional society, the image of patriarchy modelled for her in her own family unit and by her father's overbearing relations.

In the last phase of *L'Assommoir*, Nana lives like a wild thing on the edge of society, out of parental and social control, and is about to make the breakthrough to that area of anarchy ruled by sexual instinct where an urchin from the Goutte-d'Or can catch the fancy of a titled or wealthy patron and embark on the career of a Second Empire courtesan. As Zola makes clear in his preliminary plan for carrying her story forward in *Nana*, this will not be difficult. Contemporary society appeared to have been taken over by sexual activity: the subject of the novel was, he announced, 'A whole society hurling itself at the cunt'. The use of the dirty word is revealing, of course, for it affirms the resented power and superiority of the woman. Elsewhere in the preliminary plan, Zola elaborates on what the plot will reveal:

> The *cunt* is all its power; the *cunt* on an altar with all the men offering up sacrifices to it. The book has to be the poem of the *cunt*, and the moral will lie in the *cunt* turning everything sour.

The italics here are Zola's own, and it is impossible to ignore the animus directed at the woman who exposes male weakness and disrupts society, at the erotic desire which she unleashes which makes men the slaves of women, at her sensuality, her 'strong female odour' – she 'smells of woman'. His view of woman is that she is alien to men's traditional values and concerns: 'Very merry, very gay. . . . Loves animals and her parents.' In other words, she is Other, and an anarchic force who 'follows her nature', who is unstable, 'always thinking of something new', a 'bird-brain' with no moral conscience. (All quotations from the preliminary plan are reproduced from pp. 11–13 of George Holden's introduction to *Nana* (Harmondsworth: Penguin Classics, 1972).

Working out of the dark, blighted and fearful areas of his personality, therefore, Zola plays up the dangers of sexual encounter with Nana, the hazards of the male erotic drive for men. And yet his anxiety about their situation could not blind him to the social, economic and existential problems faced by women. As can be seen from *L'Assommoir* he had a keen appreciation of the factors that drove young girls from the underclass into prostitution, to the extent that at any one time in the second half of the nineteenth century twenty thousand of them worked the streets of Paris: he portrays clearly the need to escape from the dreariness and degradation that accompany poverty, the crowded living conditions which mean discomfort, lack of decency and premature knowledge of sex, the poor self-image encountered in families living below the poverty line, the prevalence of alcoholism, the inability to earn a living wage in occupations other than prostitution. At the height of her career, Nana still retains and can recount her memories of her beginnings, and the presence of her aunt, Madame Lerat, is a living reminder for her of those days. Economic revenge is therefore inevitable; but what is much more significant than his awareness of women's economic and social vulnerability is his sensitivity to what the phenomenon of a 'whole society hurling itself at the cunt' means for women. Zola's own inhibitions, reservations and sexual anxiety cause him to see as obscene the merely genital relationships which his male characters have with women, and the couplings which are determined by the physical laws of attraction rather than by the higher faculties. What I think he depicts in the many, many men who come to secure sexual possession of Nana is the pornography, as Dworkin (1981) would put it, of men possessing women. The sexual act can be viewed as the imposition of phallic dominance, violence and intrusion: Zola, who had created Gervaise, was certainly aware of how it can obliterate the woman. The idea is so developed in the novel that by a paradigm shift sexual possession of women by men is seen to stand for the more general possession of women by men which, as we know, is the basis of patriarchy. It is certainly possible to argue that sexual relationships reflect and provide a critique of the wider relationships between men and women. The conclusion may well be that those relationships are wrong.

Zola always intended Nana to be the symbol of woman as a sensual, sexual being – he says so specifically in the preliminary plan – but in fact, she becomes much more than this cliché. It is she who spearheads the revolt against traditional patriarchal social assumptions and behaviour which are embodied in the act of sexual possession. The ambiguity of her position, poised between the low prostitution which she never entirely leaves behind her and the quasi-wifely status of the courtesan, and her beauty and her popularity allow her to make a stand for all women. Women who live like her are usually viewed as social deviants: Nana, known in the novel only by her baby nickname and never given a patronymic, can be seen as paradigmatic, representing all women's civil non-existence and perpetual legal and social infancy. Often seen as a degraded figure, she is the one who comes to stand up for women's dignity and for human dignity. Traditionally she would be a marginalized character; Zola will make something of this by allowing her to lead an existence right out in a metaphorical wildness quite outside familiar social and cultural norms where nothing can mitigate her highly individual, shocking and disorientating behaviours. Unexpectedly a member of the oldest profession of all becomes the prophet of new ways of being.

Nana is a heroine indeed, but heroic status is never easily won or maintained. Inevitably she challenges her creator: no born patriarch ever relinquished his status without a fuss, and it would be in vain to pretend that Zola's warning growl cannot be clearly heard by the reader. At the same time, it seems beyond doubt that he saw a question mark over the system big enough to warrant a powerful attack on it.

Chapter Two

. . . AND WHAT HAS SHE DONE?

HERE IS every evidence, literary and other, to suggest that in late-nineteenth-century France intercourse with prostitutes was part of the normal life of men (McMillan 1981: 21). Despite a profound fear of syphilis, and in the teeth of the evidence that, even with the legal sanctions I have already described, the practice was unsafe, the belief seems to have persisted among the patriarchs who enjoyed it that it was the women who paid the price of illness, pain, pregnancy and ostracism (Millett 1977: 123). Often the women did, of course; no one examined the men to assess the health of their urino-genitary tracts. Pregnancy was frequent among prostitutes, according to Jill Harsin (1985: 118). Moreover, the whole system was built on a double standard of behaviour which allowed men a degree of sexual freedom not allowed to women. Inevitably women must have resented their situation and dreamed of revenge; in contemporary literature, they sometimes manage to exact it, like Irma, the patient in Guy de Maupassant's *Bed No. 29* (1970: 158–71), who deliberately took it upon herself to spread syphilis through her clients from the hated Prussian army – and here, of course, the revenge has an added dimension because of the clients' provenance – or as in *Le Voleur*, the novel by Georges Darien (1898), where the attack is aimed at the hypocrisy and depravity of bourgeois morality, and the prostitute is the avenger of working-class women (McMillan 1981: 22).

In his discussion of this point, James F. McMillan draws a

parallel between *Le Voleur* and *Nana* because the latter, too, is a novel about the prostitute as an instrument of class vengeance. The parallel is valid, of course, but I think that the uniqueness of *Nana* needs to be pointed out, and can be best appreciated in the light of his own comment that for women of that period the inequalities of class were exacerbated by those of sex (McMillan 1981: 24).

Nana's revenge takes the lot on board, to such an extent that it is sometimes quite difficult to separate the strands. Her on-slaught is on the whole patriarchal system, and she flouts every single patriarchal value, frustrates every patriarchal expectation and even apparently annexes patriarchal ways of being and behaving for herself. Moreover, unlike Maupassant's Irma, who can shout with triumph on her death-bed, 'I had my revenge!', Nana is quite unaware of what she is doing as she goes along, or of what she has accomplished in the end. Whatever she does, she does unconsciously, unintentionally, writes Zola in the preliminary material for the novel.

> Follows her nature, but never does harm for harm's sake, and feels sorry for people. . . . Tomorrow doesn't exist. . . . ends up regarding man as a material to exploit, becoming a force of Nature, a ferment of destruction, but without meaning to, . . . destroying everything she approaches, and turning society sour just as women having a period turn milk sour. . . . She instinctively makes a rush for pleasure and possessions.

And therefore, whatever happens, she simply can't help it. My feminist instincts tend to rebel here at what can be seen as the demotion or belittling of a fully adult woman. Ever since Eve was marginalized for having no conscience or consciousness of right and wrong, there have been innumerable variants on the anarchic, amoral, stupid female prototype, and I suspect that Nana could be another. I also wonder whether Zola cannot face the implications of creating a 'real' woman character; I have misgivings about authors who place on women heavy symbolic burdens which obscure their humanity. The link between Nana's destabilizing of society and the offensive belief about the baleful effects caused by menstruating women seems to confirm my view that Zola approaches Nana and what she does through an anti-feminist optic.

At the same time, however, I can see how Nana's lack of a conscience, ability to follow her instincts and unconscious responses, and even the absence of an explicit logic to her actions make her effect much more powerful. Zola's decision, which he announces in the plan, simply to pick Nana up as a character without giving many explicit details about her past also seems to have a point as it leaves the field for her revenge much more open. If she is 'mindless', she is in fact to be seen as a *tabula rasa*, free from all acquired modes of thinking and behaving. If Nana were to be characterized as a sentient adult woman who had to evolve a plan and execute it through all the stages of dilemma and indecision, she would have to work through such a weight of internalized prohibition, and would be so keenly aware of her 'immorality' and lack of honour and integrity that she would never achieve what she does. As it is, Nana takes on as no mere 'character' could the whole problem of patriarchal male–female relationships – ownership, possession, authority and control of women by men – which begins with control over women's bodies and who has physical access to them (Dworkin 1981: 203).

As I have said earlier, the sexual act more than any other can be seen as destroying women's 'separateness', their integrity and identity. In the case of the prostitute, the issue is acute: recourse to sex with prostitutes is for men often an exploitative off-loading of unresolved personal conflicts and problems, so that the woman becomes a fantasy figure which denies her human reality. For the prostitute, the sale of her body alone is a denial of her complex humanity. Appropriately this is where Nana comes in: at the beginning of the novel, Nana, the prostitute whose star is rising, who would be expected to be instantly sexually available, disappoints all such expectations.

The very first time we see her at the *Variétés* she is the ultimate object of the sexual fantasy of males who use her name as familiarly as they would like to use her body; on stage she is the incarnation of female beauty which every man in the theatre would like to possess. Yet what Nana's stance indicates is that she is inaccessible and that this is her power; like Angela Carter's parody of her, the winged aerialist Fevvers in *Nights at the Circus*, it is she who imposes the rules:

> Look at me! With a grand, proud, ironic grace she exhibited herself before the audience as if she were a marvellous present, too good to be played with. Look, not touch. She was twice as large as life, and as succinctly finite as any object that is intended to be seen, not handled. Look! Hands off! LOOK AT ME!
>
> (Carter 1984: 15)

The rest of the description amplifies the idea. Nana's naked body – shoulders, breasts, hips, thighs – is evoked as if in a *blason* (Hamon 1983: 174), the poetic form which expresses male sexual frustration. The notion of challenge or offensive is contained in the reference to her 'Amazon breasts, the rosy points of which stood up as stiff and straight as spears'; the involuntary stiffening of erectile tissue conveys the fierce anti-maleness of the Amazon. Her very smile is not the normal piece of body language which denotes welcome and willingness to enter into relationship, but that of an indifferent sphinx about to turn man-eater; man-eating animals, of course, merely follow their internal, instinctive promptings.

The whole scene at the *Variétés* mimics the pattern of the sex act from initial attraction – 'There was no denying she was an amusing creature, this lovely girl' (*33*) – to the height of excitement – 'Backs arched and quivered as if unseen violin-bows had been drawn back across their muscles; and on the nape of many a neck the down stirred in the hot, stray breath from some woman's lips' (*46*) – and even to post-coital let-down – 'the auditorium, lately so full of heat and noise, suddenly fell into a heavy sleep' (*47*). What is missing is, of course, penetration. No wonder Nana's college-boy admirer, rushing with burning cheeks towards the vaginal Passage des Panoramas, which gives access to the stage-door and to Nana, finds its gate closed and his way barred, so that he has to leave with tears of impotent desire in his eyes. It is not surprising, either, that Zola describes her constantly here in terms of power, conquest and triumph.

What has to be understood is that the millennia-old thought-patterns and behavioural codes of patriarchy are so deeply imprinted on the men that they are not likely to be apt learners of new ways of relating. On the following day they turn up at her apartment according to accepted custom which decrees that the sexual chase is legitimate and its outcome guaranteed, hotly pursuing her and expecting her to submit to being quarried; this is the metaphor chosen by Zola to describe the conduct of the admirers who come to the Boulevard Haussmann, and it is reinforced by metaphors of siege and warfare. What the men find is that Nana will defend her personal space against them, even to the extent of locking the connecting doors between the public and private areas of the apartment. While Nana's apartment is her home, it is not in the least bit homely, and they are forced to sit in waiting-rooms and ante-rooms in a state of almost Kafka-esque anticipation and disorientation in which the silence is punctuated by the shrilling doorbell. The learning process is an experiential one, and no explanations are given; traditionally women defer to men and acknowledge their importance, but Nana's signal to men is that they are importunate. By allowing Nana to repeat the same lesson over and over again in the second chapter and intermittently thereafter, Zola shows that he is anxious for us to see clearly what Nana is doing, and the scale of the battle and the nature and extent of the casualties reflect its importance and – by traditional standards – its radicalness and awfulness.

Of all the men who pursue Nana, Count Muffat deserves particular attention, for his experiences with her serve to remind us more forcibly than any other that male nightmares spawn not merely temptresses, but reluctant Penelopes, recalcitrant Lysistratas and other hellcats, too. In fact it seems that Zola creates situations when desire is likely to be fanned by nudity and proximity for Nana to show her own indifference, and refuse to co-operate. In the scene in her dressing-room at the theatre when Muffat in his official capacity as imperial courtier accompanies the Prince of Scotland to visit her, Muffat sits with desire mounting, watching her make up for her performance as Venus. Zola shows Nana as totally self-absorbed, gazing raptly at her reflection in the mirror, concentrating on her face-painting operation. What is really going on is a totally narcissistic involvement with her own image; Venus attending to her reflection in the mirror irresistibly recalls the 'Venus mirror' symbol ♀ which symbolizes female and feminine and reflects perfectly the self-possession and self-sufficiency which is the essence of femininity (Ong 1981: 77). Zola offers us a view of her as 'the Other', narcissistically self-contained and unattainable, while in the vicinity the cats – for Freud the embodiment of narcissism – frisk and play. Meanwhile Muffat the male is experiencing all the conflict, stress and tension associated with the symbol of Mars's spear (♂): male and female are indeed poles apart here, having quite different aspirations. The same situation will recur later when Muffat, having forced his company upon Nana in the hope of reviving their relationship, invades the privacy of her apartment in the belief that she is going to sleep with him. But her seductive striptease is not for his benefit: Nana admires her reflection in the mirror for her own satisfaction. In decreeing that women's bodies are for the sexual enjoyment of men and for procreation, patriarchy has cut women off from exploring, experiencing and knowing their own bodies. 'The sight of herself always surprised her' (*222*), writes Zola, and Nana moves this way and that 'as if to become more conscious of her body' (*223*). Muffat becomes increasingly angry at being excluded, but Nana does not need a man's approving gaze to validate her; she herself will acknowledge the beauty of her own body with a kiss.

Men use women as mirrors, explains Mary Donaldson Evans in her study of Guy de Maupassant; *his* identity is fragile unless affirmed by *her* (Evans 1986: 125–8). When, as here, the mirror is impervious and impenetrable, full of her own image, she plunges him into the depths of despair. By indicating as she does by her self-stimulation that masturbation and masturbatory fantasy are a surer guarantee of orgasm for a woman than heterosexual intercourse, Nana administers the *coup de grâce* to male pride. Her last appearance on the Paris stage as Melusine says it all; by this time Zola has metamorphosed her into a metallic, jewelled, crystalline woman reminiscent of Baudelaire's fantasies of the cold, hard, autonomous, literally impenetrable female. (In *Les Fleurs du mal*; see, for example, nos xxiv and xxvii.) Significantly speech – the means of communication between human beings – is on this occasion totally denied to Nana. For in the scenes I have been describing, Nana never speaks; she simply '*is*' women's need for autonomy, independence and consideration, and their desire that men relate to them in ways other than the primarily sexual. For men to take this on board would mean a profound modification of the conventional, patriarchal ways in which men behave towards women; it entails a different view of women, for it means seeing them as human beings and not as objects of power and sexual fantasy. The kind of pure assertion which Nana models is one way of making the point, but the fact remains that the assumptions of patriarchy are highly resilient, and the world remains full of unreconstructed males – 'bores', Nana calls them – who expect to colonize Nana's body and to control her. Economic inferiority and vulnerability make it impossible for Nana to stage an outright sexual strike, but all unconsciously and unintentionally, in conformity with Zola's view of her, she manages to find other ways of demolishing the male ego by instinctively targeting the areas where men are traditionally most sensitive.

Merely to be exposed to Nana is to be exposed to feelings of inferiority, weakness and vulnerability which are women's common experience, but are experienced by men as intolerable. If, because her own fate depends on their favour, she cannot reject their demands, she ensures that they, too, get the feeling that their wings are clipped. They simply do not have the initiative; Nana makes them suffer in the grip of passion while she takes decisions, or eats oysters or even chats with her old friend Daguenet. Competition is of the essence in relationships with Nana as she makes her suitors square up to each other – and to humiliation – on the sexual battleground. At La Mignotte, Muffat who has been hanging around for three months waiting for Nana's favours finds the love-bite on Georges Hugon's neck a chastening sign, and when his suspicions are confirmed, he is horrified to think that an adolescent is being preferred to him. Moreover, an attempt to impose himself on Nana, who is

Steiner's mistress at this point, leads to total loss of face: he grabs hold of her, thinking that he can force her physically, but such masterful behaviour is doomed. Steiner enters the room, conventional social behaviour asserts itself over the anarchy of desire, sealing Muffat's defeat and enforced acceptance of the situation. 'The two men shook hands' (*190*), and Nana, having seen them both off, goes upstairs to make love with Georges. The same situation will be reproduced in Paris when Muffat visits Nana's apartment, Steiner appears inopportunely, and both men are expelled in favour of Fontan: 'The two men left without saying a word. On the pavement outside, moved by fellow feeling they exchanged a silent handshake' (*241*). This gesture is clearly a sign of male solidarity faced with this female threat. The traditional male social hierarchy is dealt a terrible blow by Nana who replaces older men with younger, more virile rivals, and prefers a student, a vaudeville actor or even a Jewish *émigré* businessman to a blue-blooded aristocrat.

What is overwhelmingly clear about Nana's conduct is that she thinks nothing of frustrating patriarchal expectations, and she evinces no regard at all for the things that normally matter to them. For her, male conventions like time-keeping which pattern and structure life are meaningless; she is late for her stage appearances and her male admirers are kept waiting. She doesn't care about the obligation she incurs to pay the tradesmen under a male-invented system of laws – how different from poor Lalie Bijard, struggling even on her death-bed with the problem of how to settle her debt with the baker. Steiner tries to buy her attention with a large bouquet, but when he turns up to claim what he believes to be his due, Nana instructs Zoé to throw him out, 'him, first of all!' She won't have any truck with this sort of obligation, and her failure to appreciate Muffat's sapphire necklace and Philippe's sweet-dish is based on the same logic. She assumes that they are trying to buy her. Patriarchy attaches great importance to fertility and pregnancy; Nana curses her ability to conceive – 'Why could one not dispose of one's self as fancy dictated?' (*386*) – regards her condition as 'a bad joke', a 'ridiculous accident' (*385*), and the baby – the son – as a 'brat' (*386*). Nana doesn't allow the existence of Louiset to tie her down, and she makes arrangements that ensure that he is reared in unpatriarchal structures and with no male role models. On four different occasions with different suitors – the Hugon brothers, Foucarmont and la Faloise – she totally rejects the idea of marriage, traditionally a woman's goal; what Nana sees is that it is an arrangement to tie her down and obliterate her as a person: 'Do you think I'm made for that sort of thing? . . . Why, I wouldn't be Nana any more if I saddled myself with a man' (*438*). Marriage is viewed as burdensome, so obscene an institution that she can literally spit on it. Her attitude to money is not so different. Money matters to men, and all the male characters in the novel are worried about it, either because they have none, or have lost most of it, or want to earn it in order to support Nana's wants – a man is judged by it and it is vital to his self-structures. Removal of it is emasculation. Nana certainly has financial needs at the beginning of the novel, but her attitude towards money, as in the incident where Muffat and Chouard come round collecting for the poor, is always ludic:

> She assumed her ingenuous childlike expression as she held the pile of five-franc pieces on her open palm and offered it to the two men, as if she was saying to them: 'Well then, who wants some?' . . . She was in a gay mood and went on laughing. (*67–8*)

Later, she will literally not understand the value of money; the sums she gets through are meaningless. Men invented trade – Nana explodes the system in a fantastic burst of consumerism:

> Upstairs, in Madame's quarters, destruction raged even more fiercely with ten-thousand-franc dresses which had been worn only twice sold by Zoé, jewels disappearing as if they had crumbled away at the bottom of drawers, and stupid purchases of novelties of the day which were left lying forgotten in some corner the next morning, or swept out into the street. She could not see any very expensive object without wanting to possess it, and consequently left a perpetual trail of flowers and costly knick-knacks behind her, all the happier the more her passing fancy cost. (*410*)

In the closing stages of the novel, Zola describes in detail Nana's relocating of economic wealth by taking it away from the men who traditionally have it; the amount of detail given undoubtedly reflects how profoundly the phenomenon disturbed him. If men were to come by huge sums of money, they would *use* it, making judicious placements and advantageous purchases of land or property. Nana *doesn't* use it, but simply spends the lot in an ecstatic, orgasmic burn-out which signifies that money doesn't matter anyway.

However, it is in her relationship with Muffat that Zola portrays Nana's revolt against the patriarchal system most clearly. Here, feminist struggle is intertwined with class struggle: before she actually becomes his mistress, Zola always stresses the difference between their social positions – at the theatre the imperial courtier visits the rising 'little actress', in the country the member of the aristocracy from Les Fondettes seeks out Nana, the *arriviste* at La Mignotte. Of course, sex and class are very hard to separate in the novel: he is inured by status as well as sex from knowing how hard Nana's life is, economically, and she has to point out energetically the realities of her situation: 'He had never given a thought to this question of money' (*238*). He needs to be reminded, even if it causes embarrassment, of the sufferings of Nana's youth in the rue de la Goutte-d'Or which were caused in part by the imperial/patriarchal economic system. But it is the feminist issues which seem to me to be brought out most clearly.

When Muffat finally installs Nana as his mistress in a splendid mansion in the Avenue de Villiers, it might be thought that he would achieve power, and with it a better sense of self-worth than that which he had had as a disappointed admirer, but this is not to be the case. Through the relationship runs a constant theme of the sapping of male power, for once settled in her new home, Nana soon becomes bored and frustrated by the exclusiveness of the relationship which leaves her lonely and without stimulation. Materially her needs are met:

> But in spite of everything she still felt that stupid, idle void in her existence which gave her, so to speak, stomach cramps. And

despite the ever-changing fancies that possessed her heart, she would stretch out her arms in a gesture of immense weariness the moment she was left alone. Solitude saddened her straight away, for it brought her face to face with the emptiness and boredom within her. Extremely gay by nature and profession, she became miserable once she was alone, and would sum up her life in the following complaint, which recurred incessantly between her yawns:

'Oh, what a bore men are!' (*326*)

Nana's plight shows clearly how successfully patriarchal structure of man and mistress (and man and wife . . .) can cut a woman off from society and friends and even prevent her from being herself. Nana will resist this process; she refuses to allow Muffat to possess her, and avenges herself on the tradition which makes a woman one man's property. She sleeps with Vandeuvres 'to prove that she was free' and with other men from her entourage when she wishes and surrounds herself with male company:

> She had long since succeeded in imposing Georges on him as a youngster who, she said, amused her. She made him dine with Philippe, and the Count behaved with great amiability; when they left the table he took the young man on one side and asked after his mother. From then on, the Hugon brothers, Vandeuvres and Muffat were openly accepted as members of the household, and shook hands like close friends when they met. This was more convenient than the previous state of affairs. (*323*)

More convenient, that is, to Nana: she ends up by manoeuvring Muffat into a complete reversal of his supposed position, making him '[maintain] the ceremonious pretence of being an ordinary visitor' (*323*).

Male meekness and submission become essential to the survival of the relationship. Driven to accepting the presence of the other men, Muffat then has to cope with the ultimate demotion in favour of a woman rival and with the reality that a lesbian relationship may be as good as – even better than – a heterosexual one. Above all it is a relationship from which he is totally excluded, and even denied the right to jealousy:

And when Muffat demanded a denial of the allegations about Satin, she calmly replied:

'That's something which doesn't concern you, my pet. . . . What can it matter to you?' . . .

Then as the scene dragged on, she cut him short in a peremptory tone of voice.

'Besides, my dear, if you don't like it, there's a very simple solution. . . . The door's over there. . . . Come now, you've got to take me as you find me!'

. . . From then on, Satin was openly installed in the house, on the same footing as the gentlemen. (*329*)

In practice, her footing is much more secure and enviable than theirs, for it is she who becomes the favoured lover.

The questions of sexual freedom and sexual satisfaction become highly contentious ones. When Muffat tries to remonstrate and reassert himself after he discovers that Nana has been sleeping with Foucarmont, Nana answers him completely unambiguously:

'Just you get it into your head that I insist on being completely free. When I like the look of a man I go to bed with him. Yes, that's the way it is. . . . And you've got to make up your mind straight away: yes or no. And if it's no, you can get out.'

She had gone and opened the door, but he did not leave. (*428*)

By this stage Nana is explicit, too, about the fact that sexually he doesn't satisfy her; what is important is that others do – young men like Georges, with whom, in the pastoral surroundings of La Mignotte, Nana who is not technically a 'virgin in the garden', will experience 'the delicious novelty and the voluptuous terrors of a first affair' (*191*). Or easy charmers like Daguenet, rough and crude men like Fontan, and so many others, too, with whom she sleeps not as a prostitute for money, but for enjoyment:

She gave herself to men suddenly, behind his back, taking her pleasure hurriedly in every corner, with the first man who came to hand, whether she was in her chemise or in full evening dress. She would come back to the Count with her face flushed, happy at having deceived him. With him it was just a bore, a tedious duty. (*432–3*)

What Nana is making a stand for is women's ability to experience sexual pleasure, in a world which appears to revolve around male sexual pleasure, and the point is made that women are mistresses of their own desires, can demand sexual fulfilment of their own sexual needs. They can even be satisfied with one-night-stands with 'some lover of their choice', an American, a music-hall baritone, one's hairdresser – anyone – and lesbian partnerships are shown to be subject to the same conditions, as Nana in male disguise goes out to pick up partners who will throw Satin into despair.

Increasingly there can be no pretence that Nana is Muffat's property; it becomes more and more evident that *she* possesses *him* as he becomes more and more enslaved, not caring to contradict Nana's whims, fearful of getting across her. As the novel develops, Nana grows progressively more powerful and Muffat and most of the other men grow correspondingly weaker, losing their fortunes, their grand names and even their lives as her fortune, reputation and vitality increase. They decline as power gives Nana a 'buzz', infusing her with energy so that to spectators like Mignon and Labordette she acquires charisma. What follows from this is a kind of role-reversal situation, as, for example, when Nana turns physically on her men to demonstrate that she literally has the whip hand:

> One day . . . she wagered she would slap la Faloise in the face; that evening she gave him a slap, and then went on hitting him, for she found it amusing and was delighted at the chance of showing what cowards men were. She called him her punch-bag, and would tell him to come forward and have his smack – smacks which made her hand red, because she was not used to giving them yet. (*437–8*)

It is commonplace for men to be violent towards women; here, the traditional pattern is transformed as la Faloise accepts willingly, masochistically, the pain she inflicts on him, while Nana finds that violence is a turn-on. She then discovers the exhilaration of other forms of physical humiliation, making Muffat play sex games which take on a symbolic significance, turning him into an animal – that is a life form below the proud

33

status of man in the hierarchy of being – or into a child, again a lower form of life, as men have been known to conspire to turn women into children. The process culminates in the scene in which Nana makes Muffat come to her dressed in his imperial court dress. Here, it is clear that the class struggle which, as I said earlier, runs through Nana's sex war, has been won by Nana; gradually her values have been made to prevail, and here her laughter deflates male pride, status, career, the manly virtues required of a courtier and the whole imperial paraphernalia, as she makes Muffat trample it all underfoot. If she looks like a tyrant and appears to work out of a model of power as oppression, then perhaps we may legitimately surmise that she is simply reflecting back what her own experience of power has been.

Only once does Zola allow Nana to interpret her actions to the reader so that they do not seem merely gratuitous. Sometimes explanations are given, so that, for example, we hear that her ruin of Steiner is based on anti-Semitism – 'She called him a dirty Jew, and seemed to be paying back an old grudge, of which she was not really aware' (*435*). Her humiliation of Muffat is clearly stated to be a social revenge:

> Every kick was a heartfelt insult to the Tuileries and the majesty of the imperial court, dominating an abject and frightened people. That was what she thought of society. She was taking her revenge, settling an unconscious family grudge, bequeathed to her in her blood. (*442*)

In each case, Nana's own unawareness and unconsciousness are highlighted. However, at the point when Georges Hugon's death is announced, and Nana quite rightly guesses that she will be blamed for this by society, she is able to speak with self-awareness and in self-justification. The development of this is interesting. Her first reaction is the conventional one of tears; Labordette, who brings the news, immediately tries to offer comfort. What becomes apparent immediately is that he has got it wrong: 'It isn't just him; it's everything, everything . . . ' (*450*) says Nana, and what she is really crying for is not Georges at all but for herself, the woman who is being asked to internalize guilt – if men are unfortunate, unhappy or come to grief, it is the fault of Eve and her daughters for ever. . . . As a woman, Nana feels that she is misunderstood: as a woman she reacts with the tears and the acceptance of a little girl under a rebuke – that is what is to be expected as conventional behaviour. Less conventional is her change of direction: 'All the same, when you've got nothing to feel guilty about and your conscience is clear . . . why then, no, dammit, no . . . ' (*451*). Nana becomes combative and opinionated – unfeminine, therefore – and interestingly, her body language is transformed: the girl slumped on the divan with her head in a cushion becomes masculine, slapping Labordette on the shoulder and smashing her fist on the table to underline her points. The theme of her justification is that all that has happened to the men in her circle is *their* fault. Nana is determined that men should face their responsibilities for their actions: 'If they've kicked the bucket or lost all their money, they've only themselves to blame', she insists (*452*). Her other theme is that society is 'all wrong' in its persecution of 'guilty' women. Traditional society is seen as having its morality and men think that to make Nana a sex object or to propose marriage to her is perfectly acceptable behaviour. Nana stands condemned for not falling in with this when she reads their intentions as proprietorial, an attempt to deny her the right to self-determination, and to force her – as she has been forced – into things she would rather not have anything to do with. Her final comment about the attraction of the life of a nun puts the matter clearly – what Nana aspires to is a life without men. It is entirely in keeping with this that her next action is to go and visit Satin in hospital – 'Nobody's ever loved me as much as her' (*452*).

Zola portrays here the extent of Nana's revolt, the injustice of society organized by males and the depth of the dichotomy between male and female views. And yet Labordette, who witnesses this scene in its entirety, and Mignon who enters towards the end, 'could understand', writes Zola (*452*). What they understand, and indeed respect, are Nana's courage and independence and authority here. As males they recognize and respond to typically male qualities – Nana is even allowed on this occasion to demonstrate her power to reason which leaves Labordette 'thoroughly convinced'. Of course Zola intended Nana to be Woman, but what is interesting is that he seems to be considering as in *L'Assommoir* the co-existence of masculine and feminine characteristics in the psyche of one individual. In fact, throughout the novel and in many different ways Nana shows many characteristics which are traditionally thought of as male ones. Much is made of the fact that she is big and strong – in our culture size and strength are often seen as male attributes, while weakness and smallness are stereotypically feminine. She is able to vent anger and to see violence as a solution to frustration in her exasperation, for example, with the client found for her by La Tricon who detains her when she would rather be somewhere else. She has ambition, wanting to rise socially, and to achieve a career in the theatre where she wants to choose her own part and not be dictated to. She has courage. She owns to a sense of honour just like a male aristocrat's. She is a leader in her peer group and, indeed, of society and may even be seen as a pioneer figure. At the races, she will disdain the full crinolines of traditional female dress and dress in a style modelled on the male jockey's silks. Her very language, in its authoritativeness and vigour, can be heard as male: Nana makes great use of the imperative, the authentic language of command: 'Chuck 'em all out!' (*64*) 'Now, get a move on, and shove the others down the stairs!' (*69*) Her exchanges with Muffat clearly illustrate this nana-lect.

What Zola seems to portray in Nana is an androgyne; she is, I think, to be seen as the 'One Which contains the Two', as June Singer puts it, a biological woman having the full range of human characteristics within herself and able to manifest and draw on them all (Singer 1977: 20). That is what it means to be fully human. Those who are fully human must, of course, be treated as such, with full recognition of their needs and feelings. The co-existence of masculine and feminine qualities in all people has become a psychological commonplace since Jung, but, despite the fact that patriarchy had expunged the androgyne from consciousness for centuries because it threatened the notion of exclusively male dominance, Zola has accessed it, and makes it the basis of Nana's revenge, which is not banal but radical. For once its truth is perceived, and its logic followed to allow men the full range of human characteristics, too, including those which are 'typically' female ones, then there are no more appropriate ways of behaving – men and women all choose freely their individual roles and modes. And the consequence is – at the limit – that it spells the end of male superiority and power being taken for granted, thus the end of patriarchy – and the recognition of the true nature and potential of woman.

Chapter Three

HOW DOES ZOLA SEE NANA?

S EEN IN one way, the androgynous view of humanity is a wonderful thing. It opens the prison bars, offers an unparalleled flexibility and versatility to men and women; it enables them to go beyond the circumscription of sex and to have access to a wide range of ways of being, thinking and behaving. Women do not have to be subservient, subaltern; men can be set free from the burdens of maleness, from the enforced need to dominate and achieve, for example. Theoretically it permits everyone to realize their full potential instead of living out of one half of themselves, and it means that all acknowledge the full range of human needs and strengths in others. (See Singer 1977: 24–9.)

But all this breaking of chains and empowering is a worrying prospect, too. From the moment Zola observed the courtesans of Paris coming out of inferiority and subjection and modelling power and assertion, he had been disturbed. Although he had brought himself to look at the phenomenon again in Gervaise, he had yielded in the end to the temptation to crush her pretensions. In making Nana break out of the Goutte-d'Or and by letting her move the goal-posts of existence 'on the hoof' in the way she does, Zola knows that he has let a genie out of a bottle. In releasing her, he has bound himself up in the dilemma which he voices in the plan: which way should she be made to go? Is it to be success or failure? Are we to feel approval or disapproval? Fear or admiration? Or comprehension?

The novel not only tells the story of Nana, but also tells the story of Zola's struggle with her. One aspect of the struggle is clear and that is his fear of her; profoundly scared himself, he will try all he can to scare his readers. 'Nana is perdition, she is the Devil', he wrote in his preliminary plan for the novel. The story which he invents around her is a man's nightmare of temptation, sex war and class struggle, tottering value systems, metaphorical castration . . . Zola finds a number of ways of creating panic, and the most obvious of these is the elaboration of a tapestry of most of the best-known dread-symbols of our cultural heritage. As a feminist reader, alert to the horrors of what men have done to women, I experience a recoil from the evocation of all the terrifying images and associations of biblical and classical literature by which men perpetuate and pass on their fears. What Zola is doing is taking comfort from the most patriarchal sources who reassure him that other decent men have gone this way, too; he seeks authority from them, as well, and the cumulative effect is to pile blame and guilt on Nana, and perhaps, by extension, on any other woman who dares to threaten patriarchy.

A whole series of associations links Nana with all the dangerous women who spring readily to mind. It will escape no one that in its bare outline the novel is a Fall story in which, like Eve, Nana is a temptress who enthrals her man and overturns his Edenic existence; like Delilah, she is an emasculating, weakening force who comes 'from the other side' to relieve not just one but many lovers of their symbols of strength, their money, honour and property. Like Circe, she has the power to turn men into animals, like the Lorelei with her golden mane, she is the siren who lures men to their death, like Melusine, from the margins of existence she manages to become yet another destroyer of men's peace of mind. Of all such associations, the one which Zola develops most fully is the parallel between Nana and Venus. Of course, Venus's story and Nana's are closely linked; the most beautiful goddess on Olympus had the power to make many men fall in love with her, chose as her mate the moody, difficult, jealous Vulcan, had as her 'familiar' Hermes, the eternally youthful messenger of the gods, and as enemy, Hera, Zeus's jealous and spiteful wife. What closer parallel could there be between the goddess and Nana, who causes all men to fall for her, becomes the partner of Fontan, is associated with the truly mercurial Daguenet, and finds a deadly rival in Rose Mignon? All sorts of details reinforce it: Venus's colour is traditionally pink, the colour of warmth, vigour and sensual love, and it is Nana's colour – there are many allusions in the text to Nana's rosy colouring at the *Variétés*, for example, and to Muffat's hungry glances at her 'breasts half hidden in a rosy shadow' (*156*). She blushes in love with Fontan (*246*) and flushes with passion for Daguenet (*331*). It is a colour which often surrounds her; she chooses pink hangings for her mansion, tea-rose velvet for her walls, and basks in the pink glow of the lamps. Her other 'prop' is, as in the case of Venus, her mirror. Nana's cheval glass framed in inlaid wood, the mirror on her wardrobe door which reflects her from head to foot, all confirm her beauty, but as in the legends of the goddess they symbolize an inward-lookingness, an unawareness of important concerns outside herself, and a real indifference to men. Zola makes her play at the *Variétés* the role she plays in real life, and inevitably the contemporary love-goddess becomes fused with the archetype whom we remember as cruel, fickle and danger-ous, a source of disaster for Adonis, Paris and so many more hapless men – and a source of doom for marriages, kingdoms and even civilizations. . . . with Venus, the rosy aura can change ominously suddenly: 'A faint pink glow was fading away on the ceiling of the room' (*408*), as Nana and Georges Hugon made love for the last time; soon there would be the red stain on the carpet, caused by Georges's death. Anyone under Venus's influ-ence may well end up en route for Troy; the flames of the Vandeuvres stables, the blaze of light in Nana's mansion, the red glow of torches outside the Grand Hotel, are infallible symbols, allowing Zola to link Paris, Sedan and Troy, and the cataclysmic end of one civilization with that of another.

Nana's surroundings constitute a menacing environment, especially when invested with an appropriate aura. From Olympian associations Zola transfers us to Stygian gloom. The hot, sultry atmosphere and the darkened auditorium of the *Variétés* are evocative of hell; Muffat in his box in the (first) circle is already in Dante territory. At the theatre when Muffat and the Prince of Scotland visit her, the dim, malodorous gaslight glow creates another infernal miasma, 'heavy, dense, overheated' (*147*) 'musky' and 'pungent' enough to cause the susceptible count to experience a sense of profound malaise. As he stands on the brink of a fatal sexual relationship with Nana, his sense of fear and alienation in the labyrinthine, tortuous corridors down which she is to be found lurking like the monster in its lair should be warning enough. Fauchery escorts Muffat on something akin to a Vergilian tour of Hades, pointing out the sights as he goes. The whole back-stage area with its narrow passages and spiral stairs is vaginal; as the descriptions of dirty water multiply, it becomes cloacal. Other warnings are contained in objects; there is the constant menace of 'things' falling – back-cloths, poles, machinery – like the sword of Damocles. The black cat, traditionally the witches' familiar, is to be found in the vicinity of the bewitching Nana, while the ginger tom is the easily recognized symbol of the sex-drive.

There are also times when the very style of writing 'takes off' and in an extended metaphor or simile, Zola elevates Nana's wickedness or magnifies her achievement. When examined, such developments can be clearly seen to be aimed at provoking strong reactions of hatred or disgust: an example in point is the metaphor which identifies Nana with the Beast of the Scriptures:

> Nana's body was covered with fine hair, reddish down which turned her skin into velvet; while there was something of the Beast about her equine crupper and flanks, about the fleshy curves and deep hollows of her body, which veiled her sex in the suggestive mystery of their shadows. She was the Golden Beast, as blind as brute force, whose very odour corrupted the world. Muffat gazed in fascination, like a man possessed, so intently that when he shut his eyes to see no more, the Beast reappeared in the darkness, larger, more awe-inspiring, more suggestive in its posture. Henceforth it would remain before his eyes, in his very flesh, for ever. (*223*)

A feminist reader will find its details profoundly sexist: the wild ungovernable animality about the woman, who is described as at once supernatural and subhuman; the inability to face honestly the female genitalia which is juxtaposed with a voyeuristic tour of her sensual, fleshy curves; the smell of female with its ability to corrupt. Meanwhile, Muffat undergoes some sort of magic spell which emanates from the Beast who needs to be evoked thus three times in nine lines of print lest we fail to appreciate its/her threat.

When Zola actually evokes what he thinks she has done, descriptions become apocalyptic in their details and highly censorious in tone. In Chapter 13, a single paragraph extends over virtually two pages (*409–11*), building a picture of Nana's 'insolent display of luxury' and 'contempt of money which made her openly squander fortunes'. Clearly condemned are 'vice', 'wastefulness', 'squandering', 'carelessness', 'destruction'. Images of excess proliferate: 'reckless expenditure', 'a river of wastefulness', 'cask after cask of wine', 'glasses sticky with sugar'. And the figures multiply and multiply:

> twenty thousand francs owing to the milliner, thirty thousand to the linen-draper, twelve thousand to the bootmaker; her stable cost her fifty thousand, and in six months she ran up a bill of a hundred and twenty thousand francs at her dressmaker's. (*411*)

The grand total of a million francs in a year rounds off the impression of wanton and wicked over-consumption. Substance has been given to the categorical assertion that 'Nobody had ever seen such a passion for spending' (*409–10*). But there are other issues, too, here; the servants rule their mistress, reigning supreme in the kitchens where anarchy prevails, so that society's hallowed hierarchical structures are undermined, thanks to Nana. More important still is the notion of her house as a 'glowing forge, where her continual desires burned fiercely and the slightest breath from her lips changed gold into fine ashes which the wind swept away every hour' (*409*). Ideas of holocaust, burial pit, ashes and dust, and even the ossuary-like 'Heaps of men piled on top of one another' (*411*) run through the passage to produce a shudder. But then, this passage is written for men who will react with anxiety to this hyperbolic vision of Nana's power; women hopefully will know that Nana's power is all a myth which Zola is building up. I think it very important to act as a 'resisting reader' in the face of such developments, so that we do not, as Judith Fetterley expresses it, find ourselves crying for the men rather than for the whores: we need to remind ourselves to ask whose relationship with whom is the more disgusting (Fetterley 1978: 19).

At the same time as he inflates Nana's achievement beyond measure, Zola also takes pains to deflate her utterly. We are certainly encouraged to see her as a child; Zola does his best to ensure that his readers do not take Nana seriously, as befits an adult woman. Nana is known in this novel only by her nickname which derives from childish speech, and has no surname to give her the status of an adult citizen: this, of course, is in direct contrast to the males who, like Xavier de Vandeuvres and Hector de la Faloise, have generally fancy first names and surnames *à particule* (Hamon 1983: 118–19). Her reactions to incidents which are serious are infantile; when Fontan strikes her for the first time, Nana's reaction – ' "Oh," she said simply, with the heavy sigh of a child' (*251*) – does not seem to match up to the situation. The same comment could be made on her reaction to other key aspects of the novel, like the death of Vandeuvres – 'Oh, the poor thing! It was so beautiful!' (*382*) – or the death of Georges Hugon, which she greets with 'the pathetic plaint of a little girl' (*450*), before her chagrin evaporates – 'she had had a good cry and it was all over now' (*452*). Her very eating patterns are characteristically childish: Nana is fussy about food at table and very fond of confectionery, and Dr Boutarel regularly attends her 'childish ailments'. When, therefore, she wishes to make an impact in adult surroundings, she is doomed to failure. At her dinner party, she wants to impress, but her guests are bored to extinction. In the theatre, she wants to choose her own part and not be typecast by the role of *cocotte*; her aim is to extend her repertoire and develop her career:

'Tarts, tarts – you'd think that's all I can play. . . . Well, they're wrong, I can tell you. . . . Just look at this.'
She withdrew as far as the window, and then came strutting

back, with the mincing gait and cautious air of a portly hen afraid of dirtying her claws. As for Muffat, he followed her with his eyes still full of tears, baffled by this sudden scene of comedy in the midst of his anguish. She walked about for a while, to show her paces properly, smiling subtly, fluttering her eyelashes and swaying her hips, and then planted herself in front of him again.

'That's it, isn't it?' (*298–9*)

What seems to be happening here is that having made her inferior, Zola is now mocking her for it. The criteria by which Nana's social skills and artistic talent are being judged as those of bourgeois, adult males, that is to say, by the standards of a culture closed to poor child-women like Nana. At the dinner and at the theatre, we have to bear in mind that Nana is being squeezed into roles and ways of being which, to her, are alien and inauthentic: her position here is that of all women who find similar pressures impossible. At the same time, Zola appears to be rubbishing qualities of courage, enterprise and ambition that in a male character would undoubtedly be presented as impressive.

It is noticeable that, however much Zola seeks to discredit Nana, and whatever means he employs to do so, an ambiguous note can often be detected, drawing attention to authorial ambivalence about his creation. The famous image of the golden fly, for example, is full of ambiguity. Placed in the same chapter as the passage I quoted earlier which identifies Nana with the Beast of the Scriptures, evidently to augment the over-all effect of fear and horror as Muffat's passion for Nana reaches fever-pitch, it is a very hostile piece of writing; in fact, it is interesting that Zola passes off responsibility for this image on to Fauchery, the journalist, who makes it the climax of his article about Nana as a rising young star. Nana's sexual activity is described, for example, as 'a nervous derangement of the sexual instinct' (*221*) – in other words it is a form of hysterical illness. As Rosemary Betterton puts it, in men sexual desire is seen as normal and unavoidable, in women it is pathological (Betterton 1987: 75). Of course, Nana is using her sexual activity to avenge the poor people from whom she springs on their rich oppressors; this disruption of society is described in a simile which perpetuates a damaging superstition about menstrual blood, for Nana disorganizes Paris, 'curdling it just as women, every month, curdle milk' (*221*). Then the image of the fly is introduced, apparently as the ultimate put-down, for surely there can be nothing more dehumanizing than comparison with an insect. A parallel is established between Nana's activity and a fly's revolting alimentary habits. She is 'a fly . . . which had flown up out of the dung, a fly which had sucked death from the carrion left by the roadside' (*221*). Her unconscious impact on man and on society is conveyed by the description of the fly following its nature, 'buzzing, dancing . . . entering palaces through the windows and poisoning the men inside, simply by settling on them' (*221*). At the same time, however, the paradox that is Nana, and that makes Zola describe her as the 'tall and beautiful' (*221*) plant which has grown on a dung-heap, is taken further, and this fly is allowed not just to be an object of horror, but golden, 'the colour of sunshine . . . glittering like a precious stone' (*221*). The Nana who is the Beast of the Scriptures is unequivocally awful and frightening; the Nana who is like the golden fly is also attractive, even magical.

The double-edged quality of Nana's beauty and the author's attitude to it are demonstrated in even greater complexity in the description of Nana as the nude Venus at the *Variétés*. I referred earlier to Zola's awareness of and exploitation of the dangerous potential of Venus in order to underline this aspect of Nana, but Venus represents much more than this. She is very often seen as the idealization of human beauty and love, and artists choosing to depict her can encounter an ambiguity in what they represent, a conflict between the earthly subject and the divine model; as Kenneth Clark puts it in his comments on paintings of the nude Venus, is this nude woman to be seen as a lofty inspiration or the embodiment of lust? A pattern of spiritual excellence or a lady of easy manners who has taken her clothes off (Clark 1976: 89)? In the case of the portrayal of Nana, the question hardly needs to be asked: Zola knows for certain that Nana is no lofty Ideal, and she is being 'painted' against the background of the *Variétés*, the very context of which is lowering. To work for Bordenave means living in his squalid environment, being the victim of kicks and blows. Philippe Hamon, in his comments on this *bordello*, run by *Bord*enave for the benefit of spectators like La*bord*ette, has clearly indicated the demeaning sexual content of the whole enterprise (Hamon 1983: 126).

The description, therefore, has disturbing aspects: what, apparently, we are being asked to view with equanimity is a projection of a woman as a pneumatic doll, a centrefold exposed to men's 'low-level satyromania' (Korda 1972: 108). The male author seems to be acting as a voyeur here, producing material which threatens and humiliates women. Moreover, as the details unfold, Nana does not emerge as a naked woman faced in all her human reality; as elsewhere, her long hair, her 'thighs of a buxom blonde' (*44*), the gauzy veil, convey her sensual readiness, but significantly the genitalia are missing, and so is the face, which in our culture is the mirror of the inner self, the key to individuality. And yet this pin-up is indisputably linked to Botticelli's Venus, and to the realm of high art. All the attributes are there: youth, beauty, vitality, the details of her appearance, and even the aura of the goddess. However, since all Venus-painting is, as I have said, slightly ambiguous, the association can be seen ultimately as ironic, and what is afoot here is a process of deification undermined by reification, a projection of Nana as both *objet* and object. It seems that it is impossible for Zola ever to treat Nana straight.

And yet, while I have been saying that there are many ways in which Zola attacks or undermines her, there are also a number of contradictory signs which suggest on her creator's part a rather different, more sympathetic attitude. For example as the reader waits fearfully for him to turn on her and kill her with pneumonia or syphilis, he evidently cannot bring himself to do so. Whatever he thinks of her life-style in the theatre or the bedroom, her death, when it comes, will not be the direct result of either – to that extent, he spares her the moralistic approach. He is particularly concerned to protect her from the dirt and squalor that surround her. The theatre is always described as a particularly revolting environment – it is a sewer, a ghetto or concentration camp where women, the inferior race, are consigned. Here, Nana in her cambric bodice is 'Venus . . . in her divine nakedness' (*163*), 'bare-armed, bare-shouldered, bare-breasted, in all her adorable youthfulness and fair, fleshly beauty' (*149–50*), whereas elsewhere, there are references to 'the chorus-girls' grubby underwear' (*147*), the 'acrid scents of toilet-waters, the perfumes of soaps, and the stench of human breath' and 'the pungent odour of women's hair' (*147*), an atmosphere of cold draughts, dirty water – even a forgotten chamber-pot. He even allows her at the end of her career to be 'big and plump, splendidly healthy and splendidly gay' (*453*), and to go off to visit Satin 'dressed in all her finery, and looking clean and wholesome and brand-new as if she had never been used' (*453*). He even creates for her the occasional splendid moment; on the day she goes to watch the Grand Prix de Paris at Longchamp, she is the toast of Paris society, and 'people had rushed to see her, as if a queen were passing' (*345*). Nana's story is a Cinderella tale of a girl from the slums who rises to the heights. It is no accident that on the day when she eclipses even the Empress Eugénie, Nana wears an outfit of blue and white, the colours of the Virgin Mary, herself a prototype of the exaltation of the humble. The confusion of Nana the woman and the horse, Nana, whereby Nana is unsure whether the crowd is acclaiming the winning horse or herself, is deliberately left ambiguous only momentarily. This is Nana's great day, and she is the winner: 'It was her people who were applauding her, while she towered above them, erect in the sunlight, with her golden hair and her white and sky-blue dress' (*378*). In some of the descriptions he gives of her, Zola clearly much admires her himself.

There is no more convincing proof of the existence of Zola's struggle with the challenge that Nana represents than the co-existence in the novel of the twin images of Irma d'Anglars and Queen Pomaré, the one a moralizing and frightening corrective to the other. Irma, the old courtesan from the days of Napoleon I, is sighted by Nana and her party during their stay at La Mignotte, and 'gave the impression of a powerful queen, loaded with years and honours' (*205*). Doyenne of Chamont, respected by her villagers who kneel to her, she is a survivor: Gaga remembers her from her own younger days as 'terribly *chic*' and recalls the 'dirty tricks she played and the cunning dodges she got up to! . . . ' (*202*). The vision remains long with Nana as an inspiration. Queen Pomaré, on the other hand, is a premonitory figure:

> Oh, she had been a splendid girl once, who had fascinated all Paris with her beauty. And such go, and such cheek – leading the men about by their noses, and leaving great notabilities blubbering on her staircase! Now she was always getting drunk, and the women of the district gave her absinthe for the sake of a laugh, after which the street urchins threw stones at her and chased her. Altogether it was a real come-down, a queen falling into the mud! Nana listened, feeling her blood freeze. (*343*)

The message is obvious: Nana, so like both of these women in their youth, could have the fate of either of them. In the 'peak and trough' structure of the plot, it certainly looks as if Zola is playing with Nana and the outcome of the novel. But what is particularly interesting is that in Irma's presentation there is in her calm, majestic dignity, and in her appearance and demeanour – 'very simple and very tall, her venerable face suggesting an old marquise who had survived the horrors of the Revolution' (*205*) – not merely idealization but spiritualization; and again one might not perhaps have expected from what I have said about his relationship with her that Zola would envisage for Nana even the possibility of such an elevation.

I suspect that one of the reasons why Zola spares Nana is that he despairs of the men. As they sit at the theatre gazing at Nana, it is as if to them breasts and buttocks are as odd as fins or wings, as Angela Carter expresses it; her own artiste, Fevvers, is given wings to make the point (Carter 1979: 68). Outside Nana's private rooms, as they queue patiently, Zola surely agrees with Nana that their erotic desire makes them look like 'doggies sitting around on their behinds' (*72*). I sense that he is genuinely moved by the plight of the women pursued by the morals police, with all the fear and brutality that is involved (*274–5*). There seems to be compassion for Nana who comes from poverty and deprivation, and longs for pretty things:

> She could not tear herself away from the shop-windows any more
> than when she had been a street-urchin in down-at-heel shoes,
> lost in wonder in front of a confectioner's wares, or listening to
> a musical-box in a neighbouring shop, and above all going into
> ecstasies over cheap, gaudy, knick-knacks such as nutshell
> work-boxes, rag-pickers' baskets for holding toothpicks, and
> thermometers mounted on obelisks and Vendôme Columns.
> (*215*)

Surely we are meant to share her 'repressed indignation' as she
'submissively' takes Muffat's arm. When she receives the
'gentlemen' at the Avenue de Villiers and entertains them with
stories of her childhood, it is not the men who try to deflect the
conversation from this painful topic who earn the reader's
sympathy.

I wrote early in this chapter that the story of Nana is a Fall
story, and this myth is, of course, commonly interpreted as a
finger-pointing, guilt-attributing exercise, but I do not think
that, despite some bad moments, *Nana* can honestly be read in
this way. Another view of the story of Adam and Eve is that it is
a myth about human beings involved in the struggle of growing
up: it demonstrates the need for both male and female to
acquire independence and autonomy while at the same time
being in a relationship with each other. I feel sure that in the
indignation which Zola does sometimes evince at Nana's
circumstances, and his irritation at the deficiencies of the male
characters, he is resisting the temptation to pile all the
opprobrium on Nana, and that he has more than glimpsed the
second possibility, and the challenge to growth, development
and relationship which it contains. The issue, then, will be to
what extent that challenge can be met.

Chapter Four

NANA, ZOLA AND THE OTHER WOMEN

THE OSCILLATION between fear and anger at the challenge directed at patriarchy and the sense – however dimly or reluctantly perceived – that this challenge is justified, and that it is a challenge to growth and development both personal and relational, is absolutely central to *Nana*, and is followed through on every level. In the portrayal and treatment of the women characters other than Nana, it was Zola's intention to produce a gallery of social, physical and temperamental types to represent womanhood; what he offers us is, in fact, an illumination of the female condition. Moving in a series of intersecting orbits around Nana's own, sometimes they come close enough to meet her, and at others they are far away: they offer parallels to her and contrasts, and through them, our perspective on what Nana does is sharpened, for they give us the experience of life under patriarchy. For me, they fall into four categories along a spectrum from those who are virtually unawakened to those who live their revolt. There are those who live with the system, though among them, some manifest a degree of rebellion; those who challenge patriarchy and win a sort of victory; the one who challenges patriarchy and must be stopped dead – literally – and finally, the one who mounts a challenge and appears to be crushed, but for whom some transcendance of her situation may yet be possible. In writing about them, Zola himself moves through the whole spectrum of reactions, from scorn and resentment to comprehension and sympathy, and even to where he can envisage a way of creating movement.

The first group of women consists of the large group of courtesans, high-class prostitutes and actresses who are the women with whom Nana is associated most. They appear initially to have almost everything in common. Their very names, like Gaga or Tatan, are sometimes diminutives like hers with the same symbolic significance: where they have a given name and a surname it is likely that in many cases, like Louise Violaine or Léa de Horn, these are assumed names or professional or stage names, so that like Nana, we can see them as women who have cut loose from their family backgrounds and traditions. Like Nana, too, they have to earn their own keep; they have the same problem – men. In many ways they are Nana's doubles or Nana's opposites. Lucy's hectic tubercular flush contrasts with Nana's rude health and rosy appearance, warning, perhaps, that ill-health is a common result of prostitution. The older courtesans' decline questions or casts a shadow over the young woman's success. They all share the same gaiety and capacity for enjoyment. The question of motherhood surfaces through the continued attentiveness of Lucy and Gaga to their grown-up children, and Rose's care for her sons, as well as in Nana's erratic approach to the care of Louiset. The same issues confront them all.

The same major problems, like economic weakness and need, are also shared ones. Nana comes from the Goutte-d'Or, a poor working-class district to the north of Paris settled in the mid-nineteenth century by immigrants from the provinces like Gervaise and Lantier, and the other women's roots in the poorer provinces and among the urban poor are remarkably similar:

> Lucy Stewart was the daughter of an English-born workman, a greaser at the Gare du Nord. . . . Caroline Héquet, born at Bordeaux, the daughter of a little clerk. . . . Blanche de Sivry . . . came from a village near Amiens. . . . Clarisse Besnus . . . from Saint-Aubin-Sur-Mer. . . . Maria Blond, and Louise Violaine, and Léa de Horn . . . had all been reared in the gutters of

Paris. . . . Tatan Néné . . . had been a cowherd in the poorer
part of Champagne till she was twenty. (*111–12*)

Significantly, I think, no compassion is evinced for them. These
and the accompanying details are retailed as 'brutal judge-
ments' (*112*) by Daguenet to Georges; I am tempted to see in
this snobbish, unsympathetic catalogue a reflection of Zola's
own attitude to these 'common' women who exert such a
fascination over men.

Yet what other strategies do they have for survival? It would
be safe to assume that, except in Simonne's case, they would
generally have had little formal education; this is certainly
Nana's case, as she explains to the scandalized gentlemen at her
dinner-table, whereas Georges Hugon is just beginning his law
studies, la Faloise is spending the season in Paris to round off his
education, and even the vulgar Fontan can invent and polish a
five-page missive recalling 'the delightful days spent at La
Mignotte, those hours whose memories lingered like a subtle
perfume', swearing 'eternal fidelity to that springtime of love'
(*262*) and ending up by declaring that his sole desire was 'to
repeat those happy experiences, if happiness can be repeated'
(*262*). In contrast, Nana cannot spell and needs Madame
Maloir as an amanuensis. For all these women, prostitution has
been a way out of poverty and lack of skills and dearth of
opportunity. But in ensuring their own survival – and some, like
Simonne Cabiroche who becomes Steiner's mistress and
appears at Longchamp decked in diamonds from neck to waist,
or like Nana as Muffat's mistress, achieve wealth – Zola cannot
forget that they are taking the money from the men. At Nana's
dinner party, nothing enlivens the women's conversation more
than the speculation over the foreign dignitaries expected to
visit the Paris Exhibition: Zola's description of the scene which
projects their business-women's interest as grasping avidity, is
distinctly hostile:

And the ladies, with pale faces and eyes glittering with
covetousness, craned forward, listing the names of the . . . kings
and emperors who were expected. All of them were dreaming of

some royal caprice, some night of love to be paid for with a fortune. (*114*)

Because they have to make money where they can, they are passed from hand to hand like objects, rarely appearing in public twice with the same partner. They form alliances, as Nana does, with Russians, Prussians, English lords and birds of passage. Satin will tolerate the attentions of perverts like the Marquis de Chouard, and Lucy Stewart sleeps with an oddball prince of the imperial family who, on going to bed, hides his money in his boots, and will play cards only for beans because he thinks she is a thief; Gaga will sleep with la Faloise with thoughts of the little house she is planning to buy at Juvisy to make the experience bearable: 'she weighed him up at a glance. Not much of a catch to be sure; but then she wasn't hard to please any more. La Faloise obtained her address' (*115*).

They have to compromise with the system in all sorts of ways; Caroline Héquet's activities have become a business enterprise with ample premises where her mother is her manager, where there is a price for the job and the future is planned for; in a quite different way, Jacqueline Baudu compromises by taking on the 'glamorous' title of Blanche de Sivry, losing her age, identity and authenticity in order to attract her clients. Gaga forgoes comfort and the dignity of mature womanhood in order to pass for a girl in the eyes of clients attracted only by youth. They accept with only the most minor signs of reluctance that these are the circumstances in which they operate. They actually identify with the men who are their patrons – on France's hostilities with Prussia, Léa de Horn repeats the opinion of the Louis-Philippard habitués of her salon: 'What utter folly this war is! What bloodthirsty stupidity' (*466*). Lucy Stewart defends the conduct of the Empire; because one of her patrons was a prince of the ruling dynasty, 'the war was a point of family honour for her' (*467*). They are therefore tied to the opinions of males; they dispute with each other the honour of being the most patriotic of the group; they are even anchored to history despite the fact that they have no active part to play in its public course: Gaga is associated by onlookers with the reign of Louis-Philippe and even Irma d'Anglars with Napoleon I. They are in a position where it seems that they must give support to male institutions and systems. In their state of economic and social vulnerability they cannot dissent – they are politically conservative, espousing the views of those who offer them money and protection. Even Nana herself when she is Muffat's mistress endorses the Emperor Napoleon III at one point. Of course, back in the Goutte-d'Or, all of Nana's entourage, whom she has just been recalling in conversation, execrated the Emperor, and her conformity here to what pleases Muffat – 'He liked to hear her express such excellent views. The two of them, in fact, were in complete agreement on political matters' (*337*) – makes her sound superficial and vapid, or even craven and servile.

For Nana, here, and for all of these women in their inferiority, Zola reveals a disagreeable measure of irony and contempt which expresses the exasperation of a male who, despite the fact that he is part of the system which has made the women subaltern, turns on them for it and condemns them. Yet let them show initiative, and he will condemn them even more. At her dinner party Nana looks at them around her table and sees them as letting her down: 'Her lady guests were behaving badly as part of a dirty trick on her' (*121*). What they are actually doing is behaving conventionally, flirting, jockeying for admirers, playing men's games with them. It is Nana's judgement, distorted by too much champagne, which is being mocked here, not the women's activities. The point is made even more forcibly in the circumstances of La Mignotte; there, the sight of the old courtesan, Irma d'Anglars, impresses them as it does Nana, but it does not inspire them in the same way. At table later, Nana lays plans for the future, seeing before her 'a vision of a very rich and greatly honoured Nana' (*207*). The women protest at the change in her, indicating that they do not wish to follow her. It is possible to see them as limited and unimaginative, unable to cope with ambition; but then, Zola discredits Nana by alluding to her 'vacant eyes', as she dreams of her future, and her 'stupid respectability', and by comparing her to 'an opinionated bourgeoise' (*207*). In other words, he can't cope with her; here, he seems to approve those who stay within their limitations. They, of course, are much safer, unlikely to create waves.

Of this large group of women, only the sub-group of actresses are able to make a stand for autonomy and independence. They are clearly ripe for influence, and Nana herself introduces them to the lesbian environment around Laure Piedefer, where what is stressed is, in a way, the solidarity of women together, and the sense of comfort, relaxation and well-being which is conveyed through the metaphor of the warming, nourishing food. Women need such strength to make their stand. The actresses' situation is a very threatening one, for their profession, which is role-playing, already involves a loss of personal identity, and the selling of their bodies in prostitution is also a sacrifice of full identity. Thus, in the theatre, where there is strength in numbers and a fortress atmosphere, they are able to replicate Nana's conduct: they energetically spurn the attentions of the stage-door johnnies who find themselves relegated to the waiting-room where they sit, patient and submissive, 'on Madame Bron's decrepit straw-bottomed chairs, in that great glass cage, where the heat simply roasted you and the smell was anything but pleasant. The men must be keen to put up with all that! Clarisse went upstairs again in disgust' (*163*). These men are infringing a code by not knowing how to interpret the 'Impossible tonight, darling' signals that the women send them; encroaching on the women's territory back-stage, they are seen as importunate, and as preventing the women from exercising their right to choose not to be available. But La Tricon's presence near them is significant: the threat of poverty means that their revolt can be only temporary. At the end of the novel, when France is about to fall to the Prussians, they are reunited with the large group sitting around Nana's death-bed debating their financial situation. Gaga sees the Prussian advance as certain to endanger the house she has worked for years to buy and which represents her fortune; the actresses are more hopeful:

'Bah!' said Clarisse. 'I don't give a damn for the war. I'll always get by.'

'That's right,' said Simonne. 'It'll be a bit queer at first. . . . But we may do quite well out of it.' (*466*)

Just as they can fiercely refuse men when it suits them, they can accept them, too, even when they are from the enemy side. The other women, with their scruples, are made to look stupid, but it is as if Zola dares not touch these amoral women whose stance sets them free.

The second group of women whose situation is exposed in detail is composed of Count Muffat's wife and daughter. Victims of patriarchy exist at all points on the social scale, but its effects can perhaps be seen most clearly at the bottom and at the top. At least the *cocottes* have managed to shake off the shackles of clan and tradition and all that goes with them. The situation of the Muffat women is quite different: Sabine is both daughter and wife, Estelle daughter and grand-daughter, and the weight of patriarchy lies heavily upon them. Sabine was married off by her father to Count Muffat at the earliest possible opportunity and allied – ironically as it turns out – with a family which owed its prominence to the favour of Napoleon I, under whose reign the Civil Code, designed to consecrate the family and control women's potentially anarchic behaviour, came into being. For seventeen years Sabine has lived a 'cloistered existence with her husband and her mother-in-law' (*78*) in the Muffat de Beuville town house which, when we first see her, she has not even bothered to turn into the doll's house of feminist discourse, so overwhelming is the aura of the imperial and paternal past in the drawing-room preserved by her mother-in-law in honour of her late husband. Sabine's girlish laughter and lively looks have been extinguished by the cold and damp which is metaphorical as much as real in this 'atmosphere of cold dignity, of ancient manners, of a bygone age breathing an air of piety' (*74*). The patriarchal influence of the Roman Catholic Church reinforces the mistrust of the feminine and the atmosphere of stern sexual morality. All of Sabine's life from virginity to the verge of the menopause has been unfulfilling; she is, as we see her at the theatre and in her salon, expected to be a respected and respectful figure-head for her husband and father, able only to smile and pass teacups, quite without identity or autonomous activity. Her gaze is described as melancholy, not, apparently, with the connotations of a medical condition, but the modern reader will see in her abstraction and inertia the signs of depression and neurosis. The talkative woman is anathema to patriarchs; Sabine's silences which are a measure of her conformity to patriarchal ideals can make her seem pathologically withdrawn. If Sabine is one stereotype of patriarchal society, the unsatisfied, unfulfilled wife, then her daughter, Estelle, is another – the naive, unawakened child-woman, the daughter who is marriage fodder. A man is judged by his women, and Muffat can be content when he surveys his demure wife and dim daughter; it doesn't occur to him that Sabine's frigidity might have anything to do with him, and he doesn't even consider that she might want to enjoy sex – real intimacy and sexual fulfilment have no part in the contract made between them. He has not the remotest idea why Estelle should display depressive behaviour and doesn't hesitate to marry her off to a questionable young man for his own benefit. Patriarchy does not even consider that women have feelings or desires of their own.

The snag is that they do, of course, and when these are allowed to surface the results can be dramatic. Nana's intervention in the life of Countess Muffat and her daughter could be wholly detrimental – law and tradition permitted the Count to commit adultery and emerge unscathed, and to dispose of money as he wished. In fact, Nana sets these catatonic women free and enables them each to find her own dynamic. There are a number of clear parallels between Sabine and Nana which the correspondences in their physique hint at:

> In the glow of the fire the black hairs on the mole at the corner of her lips looked almost fair. It was Nana's mole, down to the colour of the hairs. . . . [Fauchery and Vandeuvres] pursued this comparison between Nana and the Countess. They discovered a vague resemblance in the chin and the mouth but the eyes were not at all similar. Then, too, Nana had a good-natured look

about her, while you couldn't tell with the Countess: she gave the impression of a cat sleeping with its claws drawn in and its paws stirred by a barely perceptible nervous quiver. (*96*)

Both Nana and this repressed, respectable wife are daughters who have suffered under patriarchal family structures; for the well-born Sabine, the sequel has been the legalized prostitution of marriage against which her own protest is to be made, for the poor girl Nana common prostitution, for Sabine the onus of respectable life in society, for Nana the endless solicitations of men, for both women the disappointment of their sensual natures which will simultaneously be satisfied at Les Fondettes and at La Mignotte, Nana with Georges Hugon, the Countess with Fauchery. While Nana recaptures her lost childhood and virginity with Georges, Sabine experiences with Fauchery an intimacy and closeness of a kind unknown before:

> now and then, when they found themselves alone for a moment behind a bush, their eyes would meet, and they would pause in the midst of their laughter, growing suddenly serious and looking at each other sadly, as if they had seen into the depths of each other's heart. (*196*)

Both Nana and Sabine thus enter into new areas of experience of relationship between men and women, and Sabine acquires a satisfying lover, even if he is just a young man on the make.

Patriarchal marriage makes the wife a piece of property, and gives her husband power over her body; as I have shown, Nana's protest is aimed at men's attempts to possess her in every sense of the word. Nana has, therefore, no difficulty in understanding Sabine's conduct, which, to his horror, she interprets to Muffat. Women need to have their sexual needs met:

> 'The fact is . . . women don't like a man to be helpless. They don't say anything, because there's such a thing as modesty, you know, but you can be sure they think about it a lot. And sooner or later, when a man hasn't known what to do, they go and make other arrangements.' (*226*)

It is Nana, moreover, who brutally points out to him when, shocked at Sabine's conduct, he is spoiling to fight a duel to save his honour, that he is guilty of applying a double standard of behaviour since he himself is regularly unfaithful to her:

> 'you're deceiving your wife yourself. You don't sleep away from home for nothing, do you? Your wife must have her suspicions. Well, then, how can you blame her? She'll tell you that you set her the example, and that'll shut your mouth.' (*390*)

From the time of her liaison with Fauchery onwards, Sabine's path runs close to Nana's. Between them, they make short work of the Muffat fortune; like Nana, Sabine evinces an insatiable appetite for luxury:

> On her return from Les Fondettes the Countess had suddenly displayed a taste for luxury, an appetite for worldly pleasures. . . . People were beginning to talk about her numerous caprices, a whole new style of living, the squandering of five hundred thousand francs on a complete transformation of the old house in the Rue Miromesnil, the purchase of extravagantly magnificent gowns, and the disappearance of considerable sums, frittered away or perhaps given away, without her even thinking of accounting for them. (*392*)

It is in her redecoration of the house that the reader can measure what is really happening. Sabine's chaise longue, once a lone symbol of luxury and sensuality, seems to have multiplied and taken over the house which is now transformed from the days of the old countess. The select few old guests from the Tuesday receptions no longer recognize it, done up to Sabine's taste, and the change shocks them: 'And to think that he was once the master here . . . and that not even a footstool could have been brought in without his permission. . . . Ah, well, she's changed all that; he's in *her* house now' (*396*). The old guard are appalled by the atmosphere of what la Faloise calls 'the gingerbread fair' (*398*) at Estelle's engagement party, the invasion of the aristocratic milieu by people who symbolize other values altogether. All the things which matter to them –

'common sense', 'respectability', the 'solemnities' which should attend the signing of a marriage contract – have been swept away: above all, sexual anarchy prevails and women set the tone and codes of behaviour: young girls dance in *décolleté* dresses, a woman wears a gold dagger in her chignon (a sign of an adulterous liaison noted by Zola in his journalist days) and a dress menacingly like a suit of armour; clinging clothes, parted lips, shining eyes, white skin are to be seen as signs that are easy to interpret. The Countess Sabine has even abandoned the black dress she once wore in mourning for what she did not have in order to appear in white, the colour of the young, beautiful and triumphant débutante. And all this is presided over by Nana, guest of honour at the party; those who dance to her theme tune from *The Blonde Venus* are engaged in a highly symbolic act. Out with the 'ancient honour' (*406*) and all that goes with it, thanks to Nana 'penetrating and corrupting this society' (*406*), not only through its men but also through its women. Her presence has made of one of patriarchy's solemn rituals – a marriage contract – a sort of bacchanalia at which the Countess's intoxication owes nothing to alcohol and everything to the sense of being liberated. Indeed, her freedom is sealed by her husband himself, who is forced by his circumstances to concede that liberty must apply to women as much as to men: as with Nana, Sabine plunges madly into a succession of relationships, and runs away with a buyer from a department store: 'Corrupted by the courtesan's promiscuity and driven to every excess, Sabine put the finishing touches to his ruin' (*446*). As for Estelle, marriage sets her free: free not to see her father again, free to fight her own battles and take him to court for the money he tries to keep from her, and gifted henceforth with a power to turn her adventurer husband the great lover into an ardent mass-goer, an obedient puppy and an advocate of stern morality. She embodies authority; not for nothing was her chest flat like a male's.

The Muffat women win a sort of victory over patriarchy. The parallels between them and Nana are many. I think that the two of them represent the two halves of Nana – Sabine, the sensual woman, and Estelle, the masculine side of a biological female.

The scene in Sabine's drawing-room matches the scene of Nana's dinner party, both having at their centre a smouldering volcano, a woman full of unfulfilled potential; when they meet on the bridge on the way to the château of Chamont, 'The two women exchanged a profound glance, one of those momentary scrutinies which are at once complete and definitive' (*199*). Nana's comment that the countess is 'no better than she should be' (*200*), is prophetic; it sounds, of course, anti-upper-class in the context, and Nana's own conflict with society is in part a class conflict which makes her hostile to Sabine; but when the two women meet face to face at Estelle's engagement ball, it is in a post-authoritarian liberal society of which the two of them are architects, and where class is irrelevant.

It seems to have been impossible for Zola to treat these women as he treats the *cocottes*, or even as he treats Nana. Estelle terrifies him for she is not even clearly a woman; in fact, we see almost nothing of her, and she never speaks – what *might* she say? Zola understands that the countess's inscrutability masks a profound personal upheaval, and that she is, like Nana, responsible for societal disruption, too. In her salon she and Léonide de Chezelles laugh at some private joke as the solemn question of Mademoiselle de Fougeray's marriage is discussed, and it is like 'the sound of crystal breaking' (*87*). The same idea is reintroduced at the ball, where a crack in the social fabric 'was zigzagging through the house, foreshadowing approaching collapse' (*406*). Zola cannot find it in himself to inculpate her; he simply plays up the symbolism of the red chaise longue, 'a touch of whimsy' (*75*), soft and decadent, representing the opposite to the hard, upright, disciplined values, but he does not exculpate her either. While the dangers of sexual liberation can be clearly seen, Zola's condemnation remains more implicit than explicit, and Sabine is never caricatured or debased; in fact, when Zola refers to her return to her husband to live with him, Zola refers to her in the most lofty and solemn terms as his 'living disgrace'. Restraint is the keynote of his relationship with her.

However, in the case of Satin, who represents the third of my categories, Zola does not hesitate to take his gloves off. While a distance is kept between Nana and the Muffat women, Nana and Satin are close associates. Eighteen years old, like Nana, at the start of the novel, Satin comes from the same background in the Goutte-d'Or; physically, with her beautiful ash-blonde hair and her virginal face with its soft, velvety, innocent eyes, she is the opposite of Nana's golden-blonde, sexy good looks. She is the destabilizing Moon. Satin is a truly sinister figure for a patriarch; if Nana is Eve the temptress, the story as we remember it from Genesis tells us that Eve is reproved and accepts punishment for her actions, but Satin is Lilith, the 'other Eve' of other midrashes who refuses to accept blame, and will not bow down. It may be possible to reduce an Eve to docility, but Lilith is the outcast woman, 'image of the fallen, expelled feminine principle that turns negative' (Begg 1984: 84), the 'hag' of feminist terminology who makes no concessions to men, and refuses to internalize men's image of woman as meek, submissive, gentle, pleasing. Satin represents an extreme form of Nana's resistance to men, and when the two women come together, it is always as a defence against the men who oppress them and infringe their essential liberty. Satin's protest is a version of the 'dirty protest' – the state of her couple of rooms is described in detail:

> in little over a year she had broken the furniture, knocked in the chairs and dirtied the curtains in such a frenzy of filth and disorder that the two rooms looked as if they were inhabited by a pack of mad cats. On the mornings when she felt disgusted with herself and decided to clean up a bit, chair-rails and scraps of curtain would come away in her hands while she was struggling with the dirt. On those days the place was filthier than ever, and it was impossible to get in on account of objects which had fallen across the doorways. (*253–4*)

Dirt and disorder seem to be Satin's act of defiance against men and the conventions of society which make women kept creatures and housewives. The thought of taking care of the place to please her landlord riles her to the extent that she becomes violent, causing her to 'shout "Gee up!" and kick the sides of the wardrobe and the chest of drawers until they creaked in protest' (*254*).

Satin and Nana are each other's companions in their struggle with men. I have already commented on the inertia of the Muffat women and the same problem seems to affect Satin although it manifests itself differently – Satin spends her days in bed. The point being made is the same one, however; just as Sabine and Estelle are nothing without the Count and his entourage and the activity this engenders, Satin exists only for men to use her and has no activity without them. That this situation puts her in an ambiguous position is obvious. On the one hand, she and Nana share their experiences of 'the beast-liness of men' (*254*), lying with their cigarettes and absinthe on Satin's bed, amid the dirty clothes and unemptied basins. When they are depressed, they support each other; with Satin, Nana can talk fluently about her problems with Fontan, and yet in fact, the women are depicted as thriving on problems, violence and cruelty:

> Both of them revelled in these anecdotes about slaps and punches, and delighted in recounting the same stupid incidents a hundred times or more, abandoning themselves to the sort of languorous, pleasurable weariness which followed the thrash-ings they talked of. (*255*)

Women bound to violent men do not necessarily seek to escape and cruelty exerts its own magnetism; here, Zola seems to be indulging in that form of defensive male rationalizing which allows women to go on being beaten. Satin's relationship with Nana is a close, tender and protective one; she is the streetwise prostitute who finds the best beats, makes her aware of the debauchery of society:

> there was no such thing as virtue left, was there, she used to say when she was talking seriously. From the top of the social ladder to the bottom, everybody was at it! . . . ordinary folk going at it hammer and tongs, and quite a few nobs, here and there, wallowing in the filth even deeper than the rest. This made [Nana's] education complete. (*273*)

Satin is able to articulate how cruel, repressive and immoral men are, and to discredit them utterly. Above all, she protects Nana from the morals police. Their repressive activities are described in detail: their arrests of innocent women in the hope of earning bonuses, the fear of denunciation, the horrors of Saint-Lazare, the hospital where medical checks were made: 'Nana listened to these stories in growing terror. She had always been afraid of the Law, that unknown power, that instrument of male vengeance which could wipe her out without anybody in the world lifting a finger to defend her' (*274*). In fact Satin will allow herself heroically to be carted off to Saint-Lazare and let Nana escape when the police raid her premises in the rue de Laval.

It is, of course, with Satin's encouragement that their closeness and intimacy turns into a lesbian relationship. She introduces Nana to the house of Laure Piedefer, which Nana first finds disgusting, but later frequents. While the novel shows the tyranny of lesbian love, the real horror of it is seen to be the challenge which it presents to men, who cannot compete with the bond of personal history, social class, passion for one another and hostility towards the male sex which sets up the women against them:

> the two women plunged into an orgy of reminiscences. They used to have frequent fits of chattering of this kind when a sudden urge to stir up the mud of their childhood would take hold of them; and these fits always occurred when men were present, as if they were giving way to a burning desire to smear them with the dung on which they had grown to womanhood. The gentlemen turned pale visibly and exchanged embarrassed looks. (*333*)

Against such concerted opposition the men inevitably lose: 'the two women sat face to face, exchanging tender glances, triumphant and supreme in the tranquil abuse of their sex and their open contempt of the male' (*335*). A lesbian love affair will be seen to run the same course as many a heterosexual one – and to run the same dangers of possessiveness and jealousy, yet after the death of Georges Hugon, when Nana knows that the world will condemn her, she admits her debt to Satin, now on her death-bed: 'Nobody's ever loved me as much as her. Oh, they're right when they say that men are heartless. . . . I'll ask to see her. I want to give her a kiss' (*452*). In other words, the love of men is worth nothing compared with the love of women – that is where the real bond lies.

Satin/Lilith cannot be allowed to get away with such *lèse-majesté*. Zola misses no opportunity to show her as a dirty, promiscuous, unreliable slut existing on the margins of society, in order to discredit her. Starting from the same point as Nana, she shares part of Nana's personal odyssey through the low prostitution of the back streets; in her, hostility to men, disillusion with them and fidelity to other women in the same position and adhesion to the class struggle achieve their highest point in the novel. She is much more extreme than Nana in her attitudes and even becomes a guide and mentor – Zola treats this aspect of the relationship in an ambiguous way, with the emphasis falling on its squalor rather than its compassion, because the danger of it is that Satin will take over, and that Nana will simply become, like her, a 'cracked' outlaw (*433*) rather than a powerful symbol of protest. Her lesbianism is the aspect he most dreads, and he is very careful to ensure that Nana remains bisexual. When he metes out to Satin the ultimate punishment, the death agony, he makes it clear that lesbian activity has caused her to die: 'Madame Robert had reduced her to such a pitiful condition' (*449*) and he has it take place, not like Nana's at the Grand Hotel, but at the Lariboisière hospital, a stone's throw from the rue Polonceau and the Goutte-d'Or. The Satins of this world must at all costs be kept under – anything which might suggest success is taboo.

On the other hand, Zola's treatment of Rose Mignon, the last of these examples of women characters, seems positively compassionate. In Rose's situation we are shown particularly clearly the insensitive, domineering oppression of patriarchy. Rose is an interesting physical contrast to Nana, being thin, dark and boyish; in the milieu in which they live, they are often rivals as actresses and as sex partners. At the root of their rivalry is the interference of Rose's husband whose relationship with her is no longer sexual but financial. Rose's experience is to be that she has exchanged one kind of male tyranny for another when she allows her lover to become the manager of her career. His aim is to use her talents in bed and on the boards to consolidate a fortune, in patriarchal fashion, for his two sons. Rose, therefore, is a commodity, and has to take the lovers who can best be milked, not the ones she personally fancies; Mignon thinks nothing of trading his wife to the highest, but possibly most repellent bidder and stoops to all sorts of subterfuges to cement relationships with them: Rose is often, therefore, degraded despite herself. It causes her anger, and creates an undercurrent of rebellion. When she decides to follow her own mind and begin a relationship with Fauchery, initially to encourage the journalist to write an article publicizing her in order to advance her career, but also to satisfy her sexual instincts, Mignon is displeased, but decides to turn a blind eye:

> Rose was out of her mind. As a good manager, he would have to put a stop to this nonsense. Payment had to be made for an article, but that should be the end of the matter. However, he was well aware how self-willed his wife could be, and as he made it a rule to wink paternally at the odd escapade when it was necessary to do so, he answered amiably:
> '. . . Do come tomorrow, Monsieur Fauchery.' (*122–3*)

As the affair progresses, he persistently tries to diminish and to break up what becomes for Rose 'a real [passion], a faithful, almost conjugal affection' (*403*).

Mignon has a firm sense of his own superiority and judgement, and what counts most is money, not human feelings. Accordingly when Nana persuades Muffat to secure for her Rose's part in Fauchery's play – a role in which Rose had been sure to be successful and score a professional triumph – Mignon sells his wife's part for ten thousand francs. She is utterly horrified by this unfeeling treatment of her professional pride:

> Rose ran straight to the property room. . . .
> 'What's up?' she asked curtly.
> 'Nothing,' said her husband. 'Bordenave is giving us ten

thousand francs to get you to give up your part.'

She started trembling, looking very pale and clenching her little fists. For a few moments she stared at him, her whole nature in revolt, although usually in matters of business she meekly abdicated all responsibility to her husband, leaving him to sign agreements with her managers and her lovers. But all she did was utter this cry, which struck him like a whiplash:

'You're despicable!'

Then she made off. Mignon, utterly astonished, ran after her. What was the matter with her? Had she gone mad? (*307–8*)

Rose's fury is patronizingly dismissed as 'feminine spite' (*308*), but of course she becomes determined to have her revenge despite her husband's continuing lack of comprehension of the situation – 'He made it a principle to keep out of women's quarrels' (*347*). All his dealings with Rose – and with Nana – are manipulative, and he is very skilful at engendering the rivalry between women over men which is a theme of patriarchal society, and is important because it divides women. All men think they know what will happen if 'they' stand united, and all means are fair which keep 'them' apart. Zola doesn't disapprove of Rose; what he even highlights in her is women's desire to be respected and to fulfil themselves. With her talent, she can make a strong claim. Her decision to put jealousy behind her and to support the dying Nana has several effects – it validates in a way Nana and all she stands for, and it also raises Rose, giving her the kudos of presiding over the community of women who attend Nana's death-bed, while all Mignon can do is to wave his fist in impotent frustration at his wife, who is empowered at last.

I have shown in some detail here how a number of women in the novel manifest to varying degrees Nana's own conflict with the male hierarchy, and how Zola's reactions to them vary from restraint to hatred and even to respect. The balance, however, does tilt in favour of anxiety; in the background, the problems raised by the characters I have discussed live in minor, episodic characters, too. Léonide de Chezelles – significantly boyish in appearance – is known to flout the conventions of marriage and society with total indifference and to get away with it.

Mademoiselle de Fougeray has taken the veil to punish an authoritarian father and gone over definitively to the side of the women, Madame Maloir wears ridiculous hats as a sign of independence and even of rebellion. . . . In such a situation, how strong and effective are the defences of patriarchy? The question is a pressing one.

Chapter Five

THE MEN IN *NANA*

THERE ARE always men around Nana. In the course of the novel, princes of the blood, powerful businessmen and youths fresh from school seek her favours. She wins admirers from Paris to Cairo, from Moscow to the homely countryside of Anjou. 'A man' is always to be found in her vicinity: at the *Variétés*, 'a man' who is a silent witness drinks a glass of fruit-syrup (*36*); at Nana's dinner party, 'a tall gentleman with a noble face and a splendid white beard' (*105*) sits among the guests, a symbol of (impotent) patriarchy, reduced to 'gazing silently around' (*113*) as the company and the occasion disintegrate around him. A 'young man' who turns out to be Paul Daguenet awaits the outcome of Nana's début, and as Nana lies dying, two 'men' who are gradually identified as Muffat and Steiner join the watchers outside the Grand Hotel (*458, 463*); all of these are symbols of Nana's magnetic attraction.

Yet in a novel full of male characters there is no visible hero, and the reason for this, I think, is that in looking at their humiliation and charting their disasters, Zola is looking straight at himself. If the characters represent, as he intended, Everyman, then Émile Zola is among them, and their frailty and inadequacy are his. The theme of the novel was, as he declared, 'the pursuit of the cunt' – male sexual desire – and in this novel overshadowed by his own confusion and difficulty in relationships with women close to him, the 'nastiness' of the male sexual appetite is brought out clearly by the fact that it is directed towards prostitutes, the sex act is too awful to describe, and the problem of dominance in male–female relationships is presented in an acute form occurring between patron and prostitute. Since all the men are involved, not one is immune from Zola's attack and it is very difficult to see what male model he would see as valid, let alone heroic.

Certainly it is not Count Muffat. Muffat is in many ways the archetypal patriarchal figure; an old man's child, in touch with some hallowed old tradition, an aristocrat brought up to 'an old-fashioned code of conduct, and . . . a lofty conception of his duties at Court' (*80*) endowed with a strong religious training, mature and serious. He moves in a man's world, circulating with his father-in-law, serving the Empire, talking mainly to other men – in his salon, for example – about men's concerns such as politics, the stock market, war; the impression given is that, remote even from his wife and daughter, he is immune to women. Zola builds all this up, the better to use it to demolish his creation, for what Muffat incarnates for him are all his own worst fears of passion, disruption and ridicule, and defensively, the author is harder and harder on the character as the novel develops. Of course, Muffat is an aristocrat and this keeps him at a safe distance from his creator, but there is no mistaking the fact that this straight, erect, phallic being, so like Zola in his stiffness, conscientiousness, his serious turn of mind and his cultivation of male friendship, is only a Man who is being humbled by Woman. Muffat is challenged to respond by Nana; from the beginning of their involvement, he is made uncomfortable, and is seen as gauche, puritanical and sexually inept. His behaviour swings from the timid to the violent as he loses his all-male, all-powerful control. Symbolically his square-cut face with its regular features expressive of dignity and correctness loses its structures and becomes puffy and swollen, deformed by her impact and by the irregularity and anarchy of passion; he embodies sexual guilt. Then, little by little, all the other structures go, too – concern with family, aristocratic position, politics, the management of wealth – and his physical deterioration in the novel mirrors clearly what is going on on the moral level. A male novelist could well treat such a character with sympathy, but Zola hates Muffat in the way that we hate in others what we hate in ourselves, and punishes him as we sometimes seek to chastise in others our own faults or weaknesses. As he is put slowly and painfully through the mill of passion, jealousy and degradation, he looks more and more grotesque – who could forget the scene where, holding an egg-cup in his hand, he tries to convince Bordenave of Nana's claim to the part of the duchess? – and the things that matter to him, like the Emperor whose words he quotes, the Empire with its politics and its rituals, the Roman Catholic Church, patriarchal institutions all, are all discredited by the events of the novel. When we see him seeing himself in the plucked larks and the laid-out salmon in the restaurant window, we understand that this is the nearest Zola can get to crucifying him.

Through him, Zola turns over some of the problems which patriarchs face – all of them, including himself – and which show up men's weakness and the weakness of the system. A patriarch ought to be able to subdue a woman; Muffat's inability to cope with Nana awakens a male terror of the assertive, mocking woman who proves to be superior to him, and Zola demolishes him still further by having his female boss, the Empress, reject him, too, with the withering comment, 'He is just too disgusting' (*430*). The mighty male sex drive is given terrifying and humiliating proportions, and the author returns with nightmarish frequency to situations where Nana denies strenuously that she is exclusively Muffat's and that he is able to master and satisfy her sexually. The problem is that men are conditioned to certain expectations, and they are doomed to pain when they are thwarted or fail to achieve them. Men are supposed to be hard and tough; in patriarchal society, they are harshly reared, and Muffat's upbringing, without physical contact, relationship or opportunity to evolve naturally through the stages of maturity, means that whole areas of experience are closed to him. Above all, the isolation of his young life has cut him off from empathy with women or a realistic appreciation of them. One cannot help but be struck here by some of the resemblances between Muffat's experience and Zola's own childhood and youth which was deprived in not dissimilar ways. As with Zola, Muffat's mother presided over his youth; in Muffat's case, not until he is in his forties does the Oedipal phase pass with his first love affair, which is with – Nana. The grotesqueness of the union is a powerful critique of the system. Moreover, Nana dismantles all of his structures, forcing him into a situation where he has to leave behind his 'neuro-muscular armour' (Pleck and Sawyer 1974: 22) along with his boots and topcoat, and reveal much more than mere physical nakedness. She even makes him realize that the cause of the pain is at least in part the sexual double standard which is essential to patriarchy, but which can make men victims of their own system.

If Muffat embodies male inability to cope with Nana, Fontan is an example of a man who dominates her. Characters like Fontan occur in many of Zola's novels; they are the macho types who are able to assert their power over females who are seen to worship them. Through Fontan, ugly and unappealing and plebeian as he is, Zola, the sensitive novelist and thinking man, can protect a fantasy of control, for Fontan can subject Nana physically. In fact it looks as if his creator is subscribing to the popular male belief that cruelty works and that women enjoy being beaten and subjected. 'Full of respect for him, she squeezed up against the wall to leave him as much room as possible. . . . Why, it was even nice getting a slap, provided it came from him' (*251*). Fontan can also enslave Nana sexually as usually she enslaves men. For him, Nana leaves the theatre and becomes a contented housewife, living for a time in a conventional, patriarchal relationship; the brute has actually made it with her, and her desire for him outstrips his for her. Zola may admire him; he may well also be jealous of him:

> She was in an ecstasy of love, blushing like a schoolgirl, her looks and her laughter overflowing with tenderness. Gazing at Fontan, she overwhelmed him with pet names – 'my doggie, my duckie, my sweetie' – and whenever he passed her the water or the salt, she bent forward and kissed him at random on lips, eyes, nose or ear. Then, if she was reproved, she returned to the attack with

the cleverest tactics, and with the submissiveness and suppleness of a beaten cat would catch hold of his hand when nobody was looking, to hold it and kiss it again. (*246*)

Fontan is able to be condescending to Nana as no one else is. In some of Zola's novels, such men sometimes have major roles, a sure sign of the novelist's preoccupation with what they represent. Chaval, in *Germinal*, for example, is written about in such a way as to endow him with a terrible fascination. I don't think that this applies to Fontan. Through the period of Nana's infatuation with him, there is a big question mark over why she stays in such a disastrous situation, and Zola himself may resent the success of this gross, priapic character as well as be fascinated by it: why on earth do women prefer such men to refined artistic males capable of delicate feeling? When his relationship with Nana ends, Fontan has already found himself a willing new lover, and his sexual success serves only to exacerbate other men's sense of failure and inadequacy. In fact, Fontan is portrayed as a grotesque fool and is allowed to exert his power over Nana only for the space of a single chapter in a long novel – a chapter in which the focus also falls on the despotic behaviour of the morals police and their attempts to tame women. Fontan is quite quickly abandoned; his very existence is an acknowledgement of men's longing to subdue women and have them worship them, and it could even be that Zola is here shying away from the potentially violent, autocratic beast within himself.

The creation of Georges Hugon and the kind of maleness he incarnates raise quite different issues. In Georges Zola projects his own problem of mother-dominance; the youth's relationship with his mother is that of a son who is the eternal baby, known always as Zizi, with a frail, snowy-haired widowed matriarch who refuses to let him grow up. His struggle against her vigilance, her refusal to allow him to mature sexually, her controlling (s)mothering of him are themes treated in great detail and Zola's involvement is unmistakeable, for although Madame Hugon is no more than an episodic figure in the novel, we are nevertheless made to feel all the tension between the restive young man and his mother, whom Zola will transform into a *mater dolorosa* – the woman who weeps for her children because they are not, or rather because they are, but something has gone terribly wrong. . . . All the guilt and resentment of all dominated sons are made to culminate in the appearance of the tragic and yet incongruous figure who comes to Nana's apartment to carry away the body of her son.

At the same time, in depicting the relationship between Georges and Nana, Zola is exploring the idea of a relationship in which the man loves the woman – instead of merely desiring her – and does not seek the usual paternal dominance over her. Here, the author is torn between giving a sympathetic portrayal of the relationship, or adopting a patronizing, or even a more hostile stance. In a way, Georges's devotion to Nana is 'sweet', and Zola allows us to see that for her, life around Georges is fun, that her physical relationship with him is blissful, and that Georges truly adores her. He certainly conveys in the interlude at La Mignotte a sense of the wonder of Nana's regaining a dimension of her youth, and, miraculously, her lost innocence; but even here, there are aspects of the relationship that worry him. Nana, after all, has the upper hand most of the time; it is she who decides what must be done when Georges gets soaked by the rain on an illicit visit to her, provides the food for their midnight feast, devises their sortie to the abbey of Chamont and suggests how to handle his mother. In fact, what becomes clearer and clearer is that Georges, like Zola, has acquired two mothers in the women in his life, and when, hidden behind the curtain in Nana's bedroom, he becomes a sort of Cherubino figure, sexually mature but unable to sustain a true adult relationship, the full extent of the resemblance becomes clear.

That Georges is 'not a man' is a major theme of his portrayal, and in some instances I think Zola is quite indulgent about this. The young man at Sabine's salon 'with his bright eyes and the fair curls which made him look like a girl dressed up as a boy' (*84*), the 'innocent abroad' at Nana's dinner who is 'solemnly nursing a plan to get on all fours under the table, and go and curl up at Nana's feet like a puppy' (*119*) are not unappealing or unacceptable. Yet at other times similar descriptions suggest effeteness, decadence; after his midnight escapade at La Mignotte, 'his face ... wore the weary, insatiable expression of a girl who has danced too much' (*187*), while when, after getting wet, he has to put on clothes borrowed from Nana, Zola places a query over him by turning him into a transvestite:

> He had simply slipped on a long night-gown with a lace insertion, a pair of embroidered drawers, and the dressing-gown, which was a long cambric garment trimmed with lace. In these clothes, with his bare young arms showing, and his wet tawny hair falling to his shoulders, he looked just like a girl. (*182*)

This is, of course, a very harsh view of Georges, but Zola's problem is serious; how to cope with those who seem to thrive on not being patriarchal? In the incident I have just referred to, Georges actually enjoys cross-dressing and feels at home with it: 'He wriggled about inside [the clothes], enjoying the feel of the fine linen, the delightful scent of this loose-fitting garment' (*182*). But the very idea of the sort of 'hanging loose' for which the garment above is a metaphor becomes such an anxiety for Zola that Georges must suffer for it. That doesn't mean that he omits to show the touching quality of Georges's devotion to Nana, but it is ultimately presented as abject and silly:

> [Georges] hardly ever left the house now, becoming as much one of its inmates as the little dog Bijou. Both of them were always nestling among their mistress's skirts, enjoying a little of her even when she was with another man, and collecting windfalls in the way of sugar and caresses in her hours of loneliness and boredom. (*318*)

And, where it is not dog-like, it is shown patronizingly as babyish. When she develops a penchant for 'the healthy pleasure-loving male' (*322*), Philippe, Georges's brother, his jealousy is assuaged as a child's might be:

> 'Here, take Bijou', she said to comfort him, and she passed him the little dog which had gone to sleep on her skirt.
> And with that Georges grew happy again, for with the animal still warm from her lap in his arms, he was holding as it were a part of her. (*338*)

Georges is shown to be unable to be masterful with Nana; he accepts a *ménage à trois* involving Daguenet, and later has to accept a whole cast of rivals. In this he resembles Muffat, and he begins to receive from Zola the same pitiless treatment. He may be content just to be near her – he is even the one there to summon help when she miscarries – but while this may be seen as a sign of laudable fidelity, another view could be that he is under-employed (real men have jobs and grave concerns) and, like Muffat, unworthily obsessed. In the end, whatever the strength of his feeling for her – 'an infinite tenderness, a sensual adoration, in which his whole being was involved' (*422*) – Zizi has to be ousted by the patriarchs and by the concerns for money and security which living in their world impose on Nana. I suspect that the extent of Georges's final discredit in Zola's eyes can be judged, as so often, by the manner of his death. Once noblemen who lost face fell on their swords, but the best he can manage is a scratch with Nana's nail-scissors and an attack of septicaemia to underline his guilt.

Georges brings Zola up hard against the fact that some men are not patriarchs, really, and it is obviously very hard for him to come to terms with it, perhaps all the more so as he experienced dis-ease with patriarchal expectations himself. As he portrays the number of other characters in the novel who in various ways signal that they are not fully patriarchal – I am thinking here of Labordette, Vandeuvres and Daguenet – what exercises him are the problems of how relationships between men and women can be other than sexual, how relationships can flourish without male dominance, and how sexual drive can be integrated with other feelings. In the case of Labordette, who moves easily, without sexual involvement, as a kind of 'universal aunt' in this milieu of attractive, available women, there is only one answer – he must be asexual. Foucarmont teases him by calling him 'Madame', and Nana views him as quite distinct from the rest of his biological sex: 'At last she was free of men and could relax, for she knew that she could be alone with Labordette anywhere without fear of any nonsense' (*73*).

But most men are obviously not asexual, and Vandeuvres and Daguenet clearly – ominously – relate well to Nana, and have with her relationships of considerable human complexity. For Zola, a man capable of that has a feminine side which is made apparent physically; Vandeuvres is of delicate appearance and 'feminine manners' (*76*), rather like Georges Hugon, but, more strongly than in Georges's case, the author does not hesitate to condemn him as an effete, degenerate figure, quite specifically describing him as the last of his noble line, and totally unlike his manly predecessors. Vandeuvres and Nana do have a sexual relationship, but he can cope with not having exclusive rights to her, and can share his territory with other males while remaining urbane and civilized always. They also enjoy a close friendship, which means that he takes a neutral interest in her affairs: 'Now listen to a bit of good advice', he tells her as she hankers after Muffat rather than Steiner, 'Don't let the other fellow get away' (*126*) And, in bed with Nana, he shares with her his money worries, the desperate solution he has planned, and his hopes, pinned on the horse he desires to name after her. One senses that, for Zola, a man who is non-aggressive and open to self-revelation is 'soft', a dishonour to his sex, and he therefore has to be disposed of accordingly, acting in an obviously dishonourable way and against the code of gentlemen in his shady dealings at Longchamp, and in his equivocal death/ disappearance. He strongly censures Vandeuvres who has the full aristocratic and patriarchal tradition behind him, to the extent of making his 'slender' figure increasingly insubstantial so that his creator can 'blow him away' as the old ethos is gradually abandoned.

In Daguenet, the issues I mentioned earlier are raised even more acutely. There is a strong bond between him and Nana: he is her favourite lover and actually feels for her and is nervous and concerned on her opening night; when at her dinner party she opts for the 'sensible' course of becoming Steiner's mistress, both she and he are upset:

> seeing Daguenet come into the room she grew misty-eyed again. He had been watching her from the kitchen, and was looking utterly miserable.
> 'Look, Mimi, be reasonable,' she said, taking him in her arms,

and kissing and caressing him. . . . Now, quick, give me a kiss to show me you love me. . . . Oh, harder than that!' (*133*)

Mimi – whom she has named thus – doesn't pay to sleep with Nana, and she will always sleep with him with pleasure. They are very alike in temperament, lively and opportunist, and able to respond to each other's moods: 'Oh, that Mimi! You couldn't hold a grudge against him. . . . When they left the *table d'hôte* she was hanging on his arm, flushed and trembling; he had reconquered her' (*330–1*). However, men who relate to women pay in Zola's scheme of things the price of contamination. When Nana named Daguenet Mimi, it was surely a recognition of a kindred spirit, and it could easily be a female name, of course.

It is tempting to wonder whether Zola is jealous of this special sort of relationship, so delightful, and effortlessly achieved. The evocation of Daguenet's chief attraction, 'his crystalline voice, a voice with notes as sweet as those of a harmonica' (*219*) and 'a voice of such purity and musical fluidity as to have earned him the nickname "Velvet-Mouth" from the courtesans' (*330*) and the fact that he frequents the milieu of Laure Piedefer as a sort of honorary female, is his creator's revenge. He even has to be married off like a girl. Daguenet, who can readily be seen as a biological male who is 'feminine' and non-dominant in nature, is made by Zola into a 'camp' figure, an effeminate of sorts; it is as if the novelist finds it hard to accept that this versatile, tender, passionate, responsive character, with his ready sense of humour and shaky financial status, could succeed as he does with women, and his reaction to this androgynous being is to present him as a hermaphroditic freak; in marriage to Estelle Muffat, significantly, he finds his 'other half'.

Although in the context of the novel Zola can deal appropriately – as he sees it – with these characters who, like all the rest, represent something of his own ambivalences, he recognizes the weakness and even the oddness of the patriarchal system to which most male characters belong, and he will not hesitate to reveal them. The patriarchs are the characters for whom all women, Nana, the Countess Muffat, Estelle and all the rest are mere sex objects and potential sex partners. At Nana's, we see them as they indulge in male ritual context, insulting each other, out-drinking each other, staking out their proprietorial rights over the women. Foucarmont tries to settle a question of social hierarchy with Labordette; the idiotic la Faloise suddenly becomes mindful of his honour as a scion of a noble family and worries about the possibility of being compromised by the loss of a handkerchief bearing his coat of arms, while Clarisse mocks him: 'What a bore he is with that handkerchief of his!' (*124*). At the theatre Mignon vents his annoyance with Fauchery by picking a fight with him, and Fauchery's honour compels him to respond:

> Mignon had given the journalist a slap in the face, a genuine, resounding slap. This time he had gone too far: Fauchery could not accept such a blow with a laugh, in the presence of so many people. Whereupon the two men . . . had sprung at each other's throats, their faces livid with hate, and were now rolling about on the floor . . . calling each other pimps. (*158*)

Rose arrives at this point, ready for her stage entrance: 'Rose stood rooted to the spot at the sight of her husband and her lover writhing at her feet . . . their frock-coats covered with dust' (*158*). As Zola explains in the following paragraph, Rose fails completely to understand this combat, and it is condemned by her puzzled reaction. 'You are nothing but a set of obsolete responses', says the character in *The Cocktail Party*, expressing Rose's thought perfectly. The most aristocratic of them all, Muffat and Vandeuvres, are particularly prone to manifest some kind of atavistic reaction: Muffat wants to fight a duel over Nana until Labordette points out the ridicule it would attract, and Vandeuvres has the urge to 'die well' as his ancestors did. In sending up his stables in flames he sends himself up, and his cynical friends make short work of his reputation: 'Somebody had sworn that he had seen him escaping through a window. . . . A man who had been such a fool about women, and so utterly worn out, couldn't possibly die as bravely as that' (*382*).

The most telling sign of the fragility of the system is that women can be like men if they want, making a mockery of patriarchal attitudes. Nana reverses roles quite happily, exacting as his *mistress* a version of the droit de seigneur from Daguenet on the eve of his wedding, handing out the insulting slap of the old code of honour as her own act of provocation, as an equal. Typical male stances, old reflexes like those which make Georges act the jealous lover, or Muffat the angry protector, are rudely rejected by Nana because they 'objectify' her.

I think that it would be true to say that the men in his novel reflect Zola's quandary about maleness, and the sharpness with which some of them are treated indicates this. He is petrified by the fate of Muffat and replays obsessively all the horrible events that befall him; he is ambivalent about Fontan, although he certainly rejects him in the end; he is aware of the attraction and the challenge of Georges, but uneasy about him, too; at the same time, patriarchy looks played out, and the old order seems to be in need of renewal. What I would like to know is, is there a solution in the novel? What might it look like?

Chapter Six

CONCLUSION

'THE SOLUTION'S at the end of the book.' For me, the realization that Nana boasts this feature more commonly found in mathematics textbooks came as revelation.

To polarize is to paralyse: to divide men and women from each other, as patriarchy does, to impose rigidly assigned codes, causes pain on both sides of the divide, and impoverishment. Rationally, temperamentally, I have always felt that a more fruitful approach to the problem of relationships and structures has been suggested by those who have tried to look beyond the quest for mere dominance which has been with us for so long. 'I believe that our future salvation lies in a movement away from sexual polarization and the prison of gender', wrote Caroline Heilbrun nearly two decades ago (Heilbrun 1973: ix). More recently Julia Kristeva has advocated an 'escape from the oppressive dichotomy of masculine and feminine altogether' and a 'de-dramatisation of "the fight to the death" between the sexes' (quoted by Gascoigne 1989: 96–7). That Zola himself had perceived the sterility of stark oppositions, and that his imagination allowed him to conceive of modes of co-existence beyond hostility, and that he could even elaborate a guiding image to replace the old models full of conflict is a perception open to all who read the last pages of Nana; once seen, it makes sense of the rest of the novel in a way that no other reading I have yet encountered does.

The last pages of Nana deal, of course, with the death of the novel's heroine. Much of the detail, as in incidents elsewhere in the book, was not Zola's invention: he based his description on the account furnished by his friend Laporte of the death in June 1874 of the actress-courtesan, Blanche d'Antigny, whose appearance had also, earlier, inspired Nana's physical characteristics. D'Antigny's death had been preceded by a decline in her popularity, a period of absence from Paris, and the desertion of her rich protectors; when the end came, she was removed from the Hotel du Louvre, where she had been found languishing by the actress Caroline Letessier, and taken to the latter's apartment on the Boulevard Haussmann, where she died, 'surrounded by her women friends'. It is clear that a number of these details were transferred straight to the novel, although there are certain differences: Zola changed the hotel venue because he had a description on file of a room at the Grand Hotel, and he had Nana die of smallpox – not the cause of Blanche d'Antigny's death – because an epidemic of the disease in Paris between March and July 1870 added a degree of verisimilitude to the death of Nana which, in order to correspond to the author's purpose, had to take place as the Empire – last bastion of patriarchy – waned.

It is interesting that criticism of the novel devotes little attention to this episode, perhaps because it seems to be so obvious a case of horrible, well-deserved retribution. Her illness certainly does attract comparison with the case of Madame de Merteuil in *Les Liaisons Dangereuses*, who is afflicted with the same disease and is so hideously scarred that the effects that she bears outwardly match and reflect her inner moral iniquity. Nana's death is felt to be a sort of poetic justice, too; one critic sees her as 'preparing her own destruction even as she zestfully causes that of the rich pleasure seekers surrounding her', and implies that she deserves 'her equally spectacular downfall and death from smallpox in a sordid hotel room' (Walker 1985: 143). There is a danger of being carried away with the idea of retribution, actually; it is hard to see what 'destruction' is being referred to, since Nana is evidently fabulously wealthy and capable of an infinite number of new conquests when she dies – the women at her bedside even discuss the dispersal of her fortune; she can hardly have 'prepared' in any way her 'destruction' from smallpox. The desire to have Nana pay the price for whatever she has done can lead to a gloss on the nature of the hotel room which is totally inappropriate; in the text it is not, as details show, sordid, but 'a decent place' (456), specially selected by Rose Mignon as a suitable environment for a person such as Nana.

Zola's portrayal of Nana's death lends itself in my opinion to a quite different interpretation. For one thing, it is not Nana's death in itself which is the real focus of attention, like, for example, Emma Bovary's. The focus really falls on those present – primarily on the women friends, as in the account of Blanche d'Antigny's death, but also on the men from Nana's circle and on their interaction. In other words, on a group of people brought into close proximity by a stressful event. Initially Zola concentrates on the men; in normal circumstances in the novel, men congregate, impelled by sexual desire, to jockey for Nana's favours, and therefore as rivals. Here, the special circumstances mean that they are involved in a non-competitive situation – or certainly not a sexually competitive one. In fact they are breaking what is for them new ground. The strict social hierarchy which normally governs their relationships is banished: the grief-stricken Muffat has no greater status in this scene than his ex-rival, the proletarian Fontan. The enmity which once separated Fauchery and Mignon is dissolved – 'they were on the most familiar terms' (457) – and although Mignon, true to type, endeavours to exert his dominance over the situation, the attempt is useless. The men have no resources to apply to the situation, apparently, and the power now resides with the group of women.

In the course of the novel, Zola shows us a number of women's groups in action. Women have their own worries and concerns in their polarized situation, and the women's group is a scene of friendliness, support and self-expression. With Madame Lerat and Zoé, the beleaguered Nana can let down her guard and be herself. In her interactions with men, her behaviour may appear childish at times because their attitude and behaviour, which deny her autonomy, belittle her, and she, in consequence, tends to regress to the age they give her; in the apartment with Zoé, 'the two women put their heads together for a serious talk' (*51*). The women bond closely with each other, forming a female sub-culture away from the male-dominated, hierarchical world outside. Nana, Madame Lerat and Madame Maloir listen to the housekeeper's life-story retailed over a cup of coffee – a real 'herstory' to which Nana's attitude is one of 'affectionate interest, a sort of submissive admiration' (*57*). This is a support group: ' "Now, I've had my troubles . . . " began Madame Lerat', and as the afternoon wears on, over a succession of grogs and games of cards in the kitchen – 'that snug refuge where you could chat and relax amid the pleasant fumes of the coffee-pot while it was warming on the embers' (*65*) – the two older women pool life experiences and find that they concur: 'Madame Maloir declared that you couldn't always arrange things just as you wished. There was no denying that life was full of snags, said Madame Lerat' (*61*).

It would be hard to imagine a man in this environment; indeed, at the theatre, where another women's group exists, the men are nothing less than aliens from another planet. Here, the women have their own concerns, professional and personal, and offer each other a mutual aid society; Nana's self-absorbed ritual in front of the make-up mirror, and the feline 'secret society' are all in keeping with the inward-turned, defensive actresses. Men like Muffat do not feel at home here, and are particularly affronted by the close physical intimacy of the women among themselves:

> Two women in their stays skipped across the passage, and another, with the hem of her chemise between her teeth, appeared for a moment, only to dash away. Then there came a sound of laughter, a quarrel, the first words of a song which was suddenly interrupted. All along the passage glimpses of naked flesh, white skin, and pale underwear could be seen through chinks in doorways. Two girls in high spirits were showing each other their birthmarks. (*165*)

Physical self-revelation is a metaphor for the women's total openness to each other and for trust: Muffat and the other male visitors find curtains drawn and doors closed to them as voyeurs and intruders.

In Room 401 of the Grand Hotel, the group of women who, in Chapter 4, sat around Nana's dinner-table, 'telling each other about their private affairs, an argument with their coachman, plans for a picnic in the country, and complicated stories of lovers stolen and restored' (*119*), have come together once again. In a way, therefore, they have already practised sharing experiences. Any attempt to mock them in this activity as trivial or frivolous would be wrong, for now it is they who mirror the much-admired values – usually thought of as masculine ones, of course – of strength, physical courage and solidarity. Rose Mignon has found in herself the ability to take responsibility and to be a leader in a way that she herself would never have suspected. At the same time, they are drawing in full measure on their traditional feminine ones – their tenderness, concern and nurturing instincts for Nana which inspire their intuitive decision to attend her death-bed and to stay with her, even though rationally it would be safer to leave the danger of infection. Their sense of the fitting and the practical is borne out in Rose's concern that Nana should have as her last home 'something decent and yet not luxurious, for luxury is unnecessary when a person is suffering' (*461*). They are totally in touch with their feelings of shock and loss, and by talking and reminiscing, minister to each other in their grief.

The men, on the other hand, remain simply a group of loners in the street. They try to blot out their sense of loss, and cannot talk about it: 'after expressing shocked surprise at the poor girl's death [they] had gone on to discuss politics and strategy' (*464*). Men are not supposed to show grief or have feelings; those who do, like Muffat or Fauchery, 'genuinely touched' by events, cannot share it, and are condemned to isolation and silence. In fact, the men have become weak; Muffat, who once modelled *gravitas*, and was so straight and stiff and phallic, is reduced to a human heap. Their masculine qualities of forcefulness, competence, competitiveness and unsentimentality have no value in this situation. Just as the women have touched in on the 'masculine' side of themselves, the men are made to know that they, too, have another side. They are made to be passive rather than active; the macho

Fontan is brought up against his physical fear, the controlling Mignon against his inability to control, and despite their attempts to shore up their defences, they are made to experience truly human feeling and concern and involvement for perhaps the first time. What I think Zola is working towards is a statement about true humanity which means revealing the essential androgyny of all biological males and females, and breaking down the barriers of gender.

And, looking back on the novel, that has been what Nana's life has been all about. Unconscious of her actions and impact in life, it is fitting that Zola should imagine her staging her most convincing demonstration when unconscious in death. Nana has not been a *femme fatale*; Nana has been, in Monique Wittig's terminology (1969), a *guerillère*, a woman of aggression, able and willing to express feelings of anger, hatred, violence, mockery and revenge – feelings which are traditionally thought to be culturally inappropriate to women – and direct them at men in order to bring about the possibility of a different sort of behaviour for both men and women, individually and in relationship with each other (see Gascoigne 1989: 105–6). To women, she has modelled power, assertiveness: she has brought men up against the necessity to unlearn unjust ways and modify their attitudes so that a new code of consideration, respect and concern, mutual feeling and freedom, can come about. She has insisted that women are worthy of account. Two images confer prestige on Nana in this last chapter: those present at her death remember her as an artiste adored by the public like the Blessed Sacrament, and her streaming hair even in death is compared to the sun with its creative, generative and regenerative properties. It is right that her last symbol should be one which facilitates growth, for that was what she stood for all along, and it is what makes her truly heroic.

The vision of the androgynous fusion of qualities is strong meat for those reared on patriarchy with its male-dominance– female-subservience dichotomy. It is no accident that Nana dies as the imperial regime – of all regimes the most patriarchal – comes to its end, and as the crowds swirl and eddy, mirroring profound uncertainty and societal upheaval. It is not at all surprising that Zola 'kills her off', even cruelly, or that this novel, unlike the others of the Rougon-Macquart cycle, is 'end-stopped' – its characters do not go on to figure in other stories. It is as if with *Nana* and her revolutionary career, Zola has reached the edge of the known world and has to revert safely back to base. It is as if in fear, the same reflex pattern always obtains. It is noticeable that among those who attend Nana in her last throes there are several unsuccessful androgynes – those who do not want to hear Nana's message. Mignon refuses to touch in on feeling: 'He had abandoned Nana completely and could not understand the stupid devotion women showed one another' (*457*). Fontan adheres to his bravado, and imperialism and the sexual *status quo* still find their spirited supporters among some of the women.

The last image of the book brings the reader up against the push-me-pull-you ambiguity of Zola's attitude to Nana through-out the novel, and it faces me with my own ambiguous reaction to the text, a compound of strong negative feelings at times, and the certainty at others that the work is prophetic. It is an image that pulls together all the themes; Nana's sexual imperialism is over, as the Empire itself is, and she is to blame; with political change, the structures dissolves, as Nana's very body seems to; and Zola the author 'deals with' his rebellious creation in those last lines as no man ever could in life. Yet clearly in this last chapter, as elsewhere, Zola writes in celebration of wholeness of personality, growth to full adulthood, relationship, the radicalizing effect of a woman in her milieu, the superiority of 'the group' and women's social structures. Nana goes on exposing the weakness of 'the system' to the end.

Two of the most touching visions of the last chapter show, first, Muffat, from whose obvious suffering we realize that he loved Nana, but was never able to mediate this to her so that she could hear the message, and second, Rose, who reveals not coquetry or rivalry, but recognizes that if 'We were never nice to each other in the old days' (*469*) that was because iniquitous, male-invented social structures made their relationship problematic. Could Rose's grief for Nana even be Zola's own? Some of his acerbity comes, surely, as a reaction to the men's blindness and unreceptiveness to genuinely helpful perceptions. However, the conversion and survival of Rose Mignon has obviously ensured the spread and mutation of Nana's 'virus'; Nana's own putrefying corpse rejoins the ecological chain to nourish further growth, and the struggle of the 'nanas' goes on despite Zola's vision of despair. In the space between attraction and repulsion, idealization and degradation, Zola has succeeded in showing enough of the reality of Nana's position to call all these ancient reactions into question.

My students, whom I have questioned on this point, attest that 'nana' is becoming more and more of a neutral term among their contemporaries. Certainly its connotations are changing: the fact that in recent years an organization committed to the promotion of awareness, and to the interests of immigrant women in France, should have chosen to call itself 'Les Nanas Beurs' is an interesting sign. It is tempting to wonder whether the shift in the meaning of the word is analogous to that of 'Black' in English, once a term of contempt avoided by liberals, but now adopted by Blacks to designate themselves. Could it be that women can now see themselves with pride as 'nanas'? And might not Zola welcome the fruitful signs of a possible spirit of reconciliation between the sexes that this semantic shift seems to prefigure, and from which cultural, social and sexual assumptions cut him off?

LIST OF WORKS CITED

Begg, E. (1984) *Myth and Today's Consciousness*, London: Coventure.

Betterton, R. (1987) *Looking On: Images of Femininity in the Visual Arts and Media*, London: Routledge.

Bidelman, P.K. (1982) *Pariahs Stand Up! The Founding of the Liberal Feminist Movement in France 1858–1889*, London: Greenwood Press.

Carter, A. (1979) *The Sadeian Woman and the Ideology of Pornography*, London: Virago.

Carter, A. (1984) *Nights at the Circus*, London: Chatto & Windus.

Clark, K. (1976) *The Nude*, London: Pelican.

Daly, M. (1973) *Beyond God the Father: Towards a Philosophy of Women's Liberation*, Boston: Beacon Press.

Darien, G. (1898) *Le Voleur*, Paris.

Dworkin, A. (1981) *Pornography: Men Possessing Women*, London: Women's Press.

Dworkin, A. (1982) *Our Blood: Prophecies and Discourses on Sexual Politics*, London: Women's Press.

Evans, M.D. (1986) *A Woman's Revenge: The Chronology of Dispossession in Maupassant's Fiction*, Lexington, Ky: French Forum Monographs.

Fetterley, J. (1978) *The Resisting Reader: A Feminist Approach to American Fiction*, Bloomington and London: Indiana University Press.

Figes, E. (1970) *Patriarchal Attitudes: Women in Society*, London: Faber & Faber.

Gascoigne, D. (1989) *Telling her Story: Directions in Feminist Fiction since 1945 in Contemporary France*, vol. 3 of J. Howorth and G. Ross (eds) *A Review of Interdisciplinary Studies*, London: Pinter.

Hamon, P. (1983) *Le Personnel du roman: le systeme des personnages dans les Rougon-Macquart d'Émile Zola*, Geneva: Droz.

Harsin, J. (1985) *Policing Prostitution in Nineteenth Century Paris*, Princeton, NJ: Princeton University Press.

Heilbrun, C.G. (1973) *Towards Androgyny: Aspects of Male and Female in Literature*, London: Gollancz.

Kanes, M. (1963) *L'Atelier de Zola: Textes de Journeaux 1865–1870*, Geneva: Droz.

Korda, M. (1972) *Male Chauvinism: How it Works at Home and in the Office*, London: Hodder & Stoughton.

McMillan, J.F. (1981) *Housewife or Harlot: The Place of Women in French Society, 1870–1940*, London: Harvester Press.

de Maupassant, G. (1970) *The Complete Short Stories*, vol. 2, London: Cassell.

Millett, K. (1977) *Sexual Politics*, London: Virago.

Ong, W. (1981) *Fighting for Life: Contest, Sexuality and Consciousness*, London: Cornell University Press.

Pleck, J.H. and Sawyer, J. (1974) *Men and Masculinity*, Englewood Cliffs, NJ: Prentice Hall.

Singer, J. (1977) *Androgyny: Towards a New Theory of Sexuality*, New York: Anchor Press.

Walker, P. (1985) *Zola*, London: Routledge.

Wilson, A. (1952) *Émile Zola: An Introductory Study of his Novels*, London: Secker & Warburg.

Wittig, M. (1969) *Les Guerillères*, Paris: Minuit.

Zola, É. (1961) *Les Rougon-Macquart*, vol. 2, Edition de la Pléiade, Paris: Gallimard.